D1515942

BUILD IT

AND THEY WON'T COME

Rachad,

Or should I write M. Le R! You have been my rock of support for many years! You were my boss but very quickly become my friend, my support, my rock, a father figure and my trusted business partner. I cannot begin to thank you for all of your support and encouragement. It means the world to me! Let's turn this year in Kwik-Web and make it the best one yet! Keep on Rocking in the Free World.

Jason Charbih

BUILD IT

AND THEY WON'T COME

Unless you use these **SIMPLE STRATEGIES** & take control of your
MARKETING

Jason Chechik

Kwik-Web Publishing House

Montreal, Quebec

Copyright © 2013, 2014

Written in: 2013 Published in: 2014 Jason Chechik

All Rights Reserved. No part of this publication may be reproduced, stored in a retrieval system, or transmitted, in any form or in any means – by electronic, mechanical, photocopying, recording or otherwise – without prior written permission by the author.

Library and Archives Canada Cataloguing in Publication

Chechik, Jason, 1987-, author
      Build it and they won't come : unless you use these simple strategies & take control of your marketing / Jason Chechik.

Includes bibliographical references.
ISBN 978-0-9936843-0-2 (pbk.)

      1. Internet marketing.   2. Internet advertising.   3. Small business marketing.   I. Title.

HF5415.1265.C54 2014   658.8'72   C2014-900503-2

Kwik-Web Publishing House
Montreal, Quebec, Canada

Cover Design by:
Gordan Blazevic (gordan.blazevic@gmail.com)

Edited by:
Harmony Marin

TABLE OF CONTENTS

Market, Message, Medium 15

  Defining your market or niche............................15

  Creating your message 18

  Delivery … what mediums do you use 20

Trusted Authority vs. Expert..................................25

  Know your product or service............................26

  Position yourself in the marketplace...................26

  Write a book 27

  Start a community...28

  Answer the two most important questions 29

Designing the ideal product / service catalogue 31

  What are some of the different types of sales? 32

  Customer Flow / Sales Flow 34

  Types of Products or Services.............................36

  Repurposing Content 37

Why you need to bring your business online 41

  Having a site builds credibility...........................43

  Showcase your products / service 43

  Provide 24 / 7 Accessibility................................43

  Deliver your message to a broad audience 44

Easily brand your company..................................44

Other reasons to have a website.........................45

Building your website...47

A good site is a properly planned site 48

Brochure site and so much more........................49

To squeeze or not to squeeze.............................50

How to start building your site 51

Always have a blog..53

Where to host your site.......................................54

What if you just don't want to do it?..................55

How to attract visitors and leads 57

What is a lead?..59

Where can you get them? 60

Grabbing their information.................................64

Social Media Marketing 71

Common pitfalls with social media marketing....72

Setting up your social media profiles 75

What to post and how often to do it 77

What else should you know?...............................78

E-mail List Marketing 81

Choosing an e-mail contact manager service 82

How to build your list 83

What to write in your e-mails 85

Pay Per Click Advertising..87

How to choose the best keywords..........................88

Creating your Ad Campaign..................................92

Targeting your Ad Campaign................................93

Back Link Marketing Strategy..................................97

Common Pitfalls of Back Link Marketing............98

Black Hat SEO strategies, why to avoid them....100

Techniques to building effective links................101

Press Release Marketing...103

Anatomy of a press release.................................104

Where do I send my press release.....................105

SMS Marketing...109

Choosing a service provider...............................110

Let's design your ideal campaign.......................111

How to build your SMS list................................114

Business card marketing strategies.........................117

How to design the best business cards...............117

Where to get your business cards printed..........120

The best strategy for using your business card....121

How to seal the deal, sell to your customers.........125

The power of influence..126

The key to persuasion..127

The Karmic way...128

Selling with Integrity 130

Bonus: Ways to make money online 133

How to use Affiliate Marketing 134

Making money with Pay Per Click 135

Create more Products, Make more Money 137

How to monetize your lists 139

INTRODUCTION

You might have heard of the old quote: "If you build it, they will come", made famous by the 1989 academy award nominated film Field of Dreams. That quote was spoken to Ray Kinsella during a dream he had of building a baseball diamond on his cornfield. It has since been used in the context of business and marketing by many great authors and speakers.

You see, up until a few years ago, we were in what was formally known as the industrial age. Just before the American civil war of 1861, the U.S. congress passed legislation allowing individuals to form corporations without a charter from the U.S. government. This was a major turning point for business, as we knew it. Anyone could start a business, provide a product or service and sell it for a profit. This caused innovation in the metallurgy industry and in machinery, while also giving way to a modernized approach to agriculture.

New types of machinery benefited farmers, who produced more than ever before with little or no effort. This allowed for innovation and drastic changes in the economy. It gave rise to urban centres and an independent economic life.

More than 100 years later, the industrial age morphed into an era where the only step necessary for success was to take action and start a business, open a storefront for your barbershop or your clothing store for example. As long as it was accessible to others, it wasn't necessary to do much marketing. The sign out front of your building was enough to catch passers-by, grab their attention and convince them to enter your store. The initial traffic and the word of mouth would have been enough to earn an honest living. People living in the towns knew who you were and would trust you willingly. Businesses flourished everywhere and the economy was booming.

Now, let's fast forward to the late 1980s, when the Internet came into play and started to gain momentum. There was an almost immediate radical shift. A new era was born: the information age. We quickly saw a switch from industrialization to an economy based entirely on the manipulation of information. The amount of information that is currently available at our fingertips is astounding. The vast majority of the population is becoming informed buyers, which is imperative to take into consideration in our businesses. The revolution brought on by the World Wide Web has created an almost instant access to information that was previously incredibly hard to retrieve. Also, the rate at which we are increasing our stores of knowledge and information is incredible. A study done in 2010 by Wikibon indicates that the world currently maintains approximately 1.2 Zettabytes of data. 1 Zettabyte is approximately 1 trillion Gigabytes. If you were to load that data onto 16 GB iPads and then would proceed to stack the iPads to cover the entire ground of Wembley Stadium and then one on top of the other, the iStack would reach 4.24 miles into the sky bringing it way higher than Mount Kilimanjaro. That exercise would require approximately 75 billion fully loaded iPads and would cost more than \$37.4 trillion dollars at retail value.[1] Nowadays, we are inundated by more information and data than we know what to do with.

It isn't about whom you know any more; it's about how much knowledge you hold. It's your story and your ability to tell it to the world in a unique and compelling way that matters. Knowledge and information are the new currencies of this day and age.

You are probably wondering what all of this means and why it is important to you and your business. I am about to answer your questions.

In today's growing economy, the consumer's demands are increasing in complexity. People don't immediately trust you. You need to build that trust relationship with your customers in order to convince them to purchase from you. The best and fastest way to build that trust relationship is by showing them that you know what they need and why they need it. You can do this by becoming a trusted authority in your market or displaying that you are an expert in your category/niche. This builds confidence and eases the customer to make an informed decision about doing business with you.

Bringing it back to the quote "If you build it, they will come", I truly believe that it is no longer the case when it comes to

---

[1] http://wikibon.org/blog/unstructured-data/

starting your own business. There are over 100,000 new domain names registered each and every day, many of those hosting websites.[2] Unfortunately, most of the new website owners do absolutely nothing to market their new website. The chances of them being seen or known are decreasing every day. The good news is that if you make the slightest effort to market your website, say tweet or publish an article about your site, your site will be in the top 5% of the websites created that day. What if you did 5 things to market your website? Getting the point?

Did you know that in 2012, there were an estimated 2.4 billion people connected to the Internet across the globe? That accounts for more than 34% of the world's population. There is also an estimated 184.3 million online shoppers in the U.S. alone.[3] Wouldn't you like to get a piece of that pie and bring them to your website?

Having a website for your business is not good enough these days. You need marketing for your business to grow and effectively impact your bottom line, which is what business owners strive for. My goal is to show you that marketing is much easier than you think. It doesn't require a technical degree or anything even remotely close. A 10 year old with a laptop can do this for you and it wouldn't cost you very much.

---

[2] http://www.whois.sc/internet-statistics/
[3] http://www.internetworldstats.com/stats.htm

This book is intended for all the small business owners out there looking for great ways to increase their visibility in the marketplace, attract more prospects and be able to convert those prospects into paying customers, all without spending an arm and a leg on big advertisement agencies.

My intention is to show you how you can use the power of the Internet to bring your business into the 21st century.

You do not need to be tech-savvy or a marketing wizard to understand the concepts and/or implement the marketing strategies outlined in this book. All you need to get started is a basic computer or laptop and an Internet connection. I will show you the rest throughout this book.

Make sure to read this book all the way to the end. There are valuable tips, links and resources, worth thousands of dollars, buried within the text. Happy reading!

CHAPTER 1

Market, Message, Medium

The first step in effectively marketing your business is, knowing whom your target audience is. This will help you determine what you need to tell them to convince them to trust you and eventually buy from you. It also helps you get your message across.

Defining your market or niche

If I asked you to describe your ideal customer in detail, could you do it?

I'll give you an example. My ideal customer is John. John is 42 years old with two kids. He is recently divorced and he is the owner of a small ice cream parlour in a nice neighbourhood. John has been paying hundreds of dollars each year to list his ice cream shop in the phone book and a local newspaper, with uncertain results. When I originally approached John, he was thrilled to get started with my company. He got to work and, within a few short days, had prepared exactly what he wanted us to do for him. We sat down and gave him feedback on his marketing plan. Over the next few weeks, we implemented every aspect of John's plan and he has since taken over the reins in his marketing. Today, I am glad to report that his business is booming. People all over town are talking about how great his ice cream is and he has more than doubled his sales in just a few short weeks.

John is my ideal customer because of his openness to new ideas and his willingness to try what we had to offer. His drive was paramount to the absolute success of the project. In a perfect world, all of our clients would be as dedicated and willing to work as John.

Go ahead and try this exercise for yourself. Take a few moments now and write down a description of your ideal client. Make it as detailed as you can, including demographics and psychographics where possible. Identify whom your ideal customer is and what it is about them that make them ideal. Once you understand this, you will be able to better target your message to this type of client.

∫

Now that you know who your ideal customer is, let's take a look at his or her description and see if we can determine your niche. What characteristics do your customers have that make them ideal or unique? How can you separate the normal attributes from what makes them special?

Your next exercise is to write out in bullet form the characteristics that form your market, based on the description of your ideal customer.

As an example, my ideal customer:

- Is a small business owner
- Is in his forties

- Is a father of two
- Is divorced and needs to take care of his kids
- Already paid for marketing services
- Is very motivated and driven to succeed
- Is organized and meticulous
- Is open to trying new things
- Is willing to work hard and put in the effort

That is my niche or the market for my business. Now it's your turn. Take a moment right now to outline your niche. Remember the following: you want to be as specific as possible. The goal is to make your pond small so that you can be the big fish. You don't need to fit all of your customers into this niche. By defining your ideal customer, you will be able to better target your message directly to this crowd and you will tend to attract more ideal customers.

When you have clarity about who your ideal customer is, you start attracting exactly those types of customers into your business.

You might have heard of the Pareto rule, better known as the 80:20 rule. If you look closely at the results of your business, more than 80% of your businesses revenue comes from just 20% of your customers. These are almost always your best customers, as well as your ideal ones. Imagine what your business would look like if you only attracted ideal customers.

∫

Creating your message

Great, now you know whom you are talking to, but what do you want to say to them?

To quote Mike Koenigs from Author Expert Marketing Machines "People are like crystal wine glasses. When one vibrates, so do the others. The more raw, real and authentic your message and stories, the deeper the connection will be."

Your message is critical to the success of your marketing campaign. Just a small tweak in your message could create a world of difference in the outcome of your sales.

If you had your ideal customer standing right in front of you for the first time ever, and you knew in advance that this was in fact your ideal customer, what would you say? Try and answer the following questions.

What would you tell them about:

- Who you are
- What you do
- How you go about doing it
- What you stand for in your business
- What are your core values
- What sets you apart from the rest
- What results will they receive or achieve

Remember that your unique selling proposition (USP) needs to be clearly defined in your message. This is the answer to the question "why should they buy what you are selling, <u>from</u>

you". What differentiates you from the rest of the businesses offering the same product or service?

One of my mentors, Keith Cunningham, likes to ask the question: "What would your business look like if you kept every single customer that ever showed up to your business?" Just think about that for a moment. Let that really sink in. Feel it, imagine it. Would your business double, triple, quadruple in size? This is what a properly crafted message can do for you.

I'll give you an example by showing you my message.

> Are your marketing efforts not bringing you the results you originally had hoped for? Can you use a few extra prospects and customers in your business? Kwik-Web offers marketing and consulting services geared towards the small business entrepreneur. We know you don't have a big budget for traditional marketing. That's why our staff of expert marketing strategists has been specifically trained to be able to show you how to implement the best, most effective, new age marketing strategies for very little money. Sounds cool? We will help you bring your business online, create a presence on the web and effectively convert it into a money making machine. You don't need to be technical to work with our team, you just need to be motivated and driven to succeed. If that sounds like you, please give us a call today to see how we can help you out.

I am not talking to a large crowd in that message. I am talking to John and other people like John.

If you try and include everyone in your message, then you are effectively talking to no one, because nobody is going to listen to you. Targeting your message appropriately will attract more of the customers that produce the majority of your revenues.

It's your turn to give it a shot. Take a moment to write down exactly what you would say if you were standing in front of an audience made entirely of your ideal customers. Make it good. Make it real, and raw. Create a connection with your audience and show them that you care about them.

∫

Delivery ... what mediums do you use

Let's briefly summarize the previous section: you now know exactly whom you are speaking to and what you plan on saying. But how do you find your ideal customers?

There are so many ways of getting your message to your market! Do you focus on one until it works or do you choose a few all at once?

The best way of defining which delivery mechanisms to use is to start doing some research.

Perform market research on the Internet about the crowd that you are targeting. Do they use social media or prefer to speak with you over the telephone? Gather as much information on them as possible, so that you can be successful in your campaign. Do not make assumptions about your target market. You might think you know how they think and act, but research might prove you to be completely wrong. Putting in extra effort now will save you a lot of time and money adjusting your marketing strategy later on.

The next step is testing out different mediums on a small subset of your market. Their reactions to one form of marketing versus another could be surprising. The more testing you do, the more effective your delivery will become and the less money you will waste trying to implement it.

After you test the various forms of marketing, investigate pricing for the forms that worked well and draw up a budget. Also determine a timescale for the channels, methods of marketing and advertising that you plan on using. This might sound like a lot all at once. However, the more preparation that you do at this point, the more successful your campaign will be. Take your time and get this right.

Figure out a way to properly monitor and report on the results of your campaigns. How will you measure success? Define a set of key performance indicators (KPIs) for your business and track them religiously. For example, track things like profitability on a monthly basis compared to the previous year or maybe the number of new prospects that you are speaking to per week. Tracking your results will facilitate you in adjusting your strategy and creating massive success.

To give you an example of forms of marketing you could take immediate advantage of; I have compiled the following list. My intention is not to overwhelm you, but rather to show you the array of possibilities. Many items in the list below are described in detail later on in this book and some have their very own chapter. This list is by no means complete but hopefully you could get some ideas from the list to start planning your delivery.

E-commerce	Website	Social Media
Google Adwords	E-mail Marketing	SMS Marketing
Tele-Marketing	Print Ads	Newspapers
Magazines	Door Hangs	Podcasting
YouTube Videos	Networking Events	Public Speaking
CD Series	DVD Tutorials	Infomercial
Key chains	Flyers	Blogs
Directories	Write a Book	Classifieds
Yellow Pages	Television Ads	Fax Broadcasts
FM Radio Ads	Tradeshows	Door-to-Door
Media Releases	Gift Certificates	Business Cards
Charity Events	Window Displays	Billboards
Post Cards	Sponsorship	Cross Branding
Widgets	Affiliate Marketing	Mobile Apps

For my business, I have chosen to use a website, which I get traffic on using social media and search engine optimization. Once my visitors land on the website, I get their e-mail addresses so that I can implement an e-mail marketing strategy. I give my customers real value by producing small YouTube videos answering all of their questions. I am very active in various local business networking events and in seminars. I speak on stages to let large crowds know who I am and what I do. Best of all, I am writing this book to create authority and trust among my prospects.

Now it's your turn. Here are the steps to properly deliver a message to your market.

- Take your time in completing the necessary market research for your business.
- Make a list of the mediums that you would consider using when delivering your message.
- Test some of the chosen mediums to see which ones work well and which ones don't seem to bring any results.
- Plan the various costs involved and build a budget, as well as a timescale for your marketing plan.
- Find ways to measure the success and report on the results you are achieving.

$$\int$$

The next chapter centres on earning the trust of a target market and positioning the business as an authority in its niche. This is a very powerful tool and for most people, can be the make or break aspect of the success in their business.

CHAPTER 2

Trusted Authority vs. Expert

Trust is one of the most valuable assets of your business, since a business needs to build a relationship of trust with its prospects before converting them into paying customers. Trust is something that can take years to create and only minutes to destroy.

Thankfully, there are shortcuts to building significant trust relationships quickly and effectively while maintaining full integrity.

Being an expert in your niche is a great thing. It will help you greatly however, the only thing worse than spending years or even decades becoming an expert in your field is doing so, then having to prove your expertise each and every time you meet someone new. There is a painless alternative: being a trusted authority in your field basically means that you are perceived by others to be the authority on a particular subject.

Being a trusted authority is a game of perception; others recognize that you know the subject rather than you having to prove it. Of course, you can be both an expert and a trusted authority, but the latter is so much more powerful! In order to become the trusted authority in your niche, you do not need to be an expert or master a topic. You just need to know more about it than your potential client base and build the status indicating that you know more. This can be done in many ways. As for the mediums of delivery, the path to becoming a trusted authority starts with research.

Know your product or service

It is imperative for you to learn everything about what you are selling or offering, the ins and outs, the qualities and flaws, the use and the components. The worst thing that you can do is to not have an answer about your own product or service that a potential client would likely ask you.

Research as much as you can about what you are selling and be ready to back up your statements with actual facts.

Position yourself in the marketplace

Is it better to be a small fish in a big pond or a big fish in a small pond? If you guessed the latter, then you would be correct. In this analogy, your niche is the pond. The smaller your niche, the easier it is to become known among the crowd which in this case would be the fish.

Position yourself so that you can easily achieve the role of trusted authority in your niche. Ideally, your niche or market would be small enough that everyone would automatically know who you are. This means defining your target based on both demographics (age, gender, income class) and based on psychographics (likes, dislikes, personality). The smaller your niche is, the easier it will be to become the trusted authority.

Write a book

A great way to become trusted among your target crowd is to write a book. You would be surprised to know that writing your message and having it published is so much easier than you think. Nowadays, it can be done within less than 24 hours with the help of Amazon and other online technologies. Becoming a published author creates immediate credibility.

Just imagine sitting down with Julie the accountant. Julie is a prospect that you recently met at a networking event. You are sitting with her over a coffee, trying to sell her the idea of building a website for her small accounting firm. Julie can't see why having a website would help her business and asks you how she can use that to make money. In response, imagine pulling out a brand new copy of your book from your briefcase, opening it up to the chapter "earning revenue from your website" and telling Julie that you wrote on that specific topic in your book. Julie will immediately see you as being an expert in the field, since you went as far as being published on that subject. You will then be seen as an authority figure and she will most likely be willing to do business with you.

What's more, you can give Julie a copy of your book for free to keep. The costs of printing are negligible, and using a book as a tool for self-promotion is much more effective than using good old fashioned business cards.

Most people discard business cards or store them in a shoebox, in the depths of a closet, never to be seen again. Now, have you ever heard of anyone throwing out a book? The average book ends up on a shelf, or is lent to a friend that will never return it, but rarely finds itself in the garbage can.

Start a community

It is estimated that there are over 128 million Facebook users in the United States alone and over 1 billion worldwide.[4] If you could position yourself in such a way as to get a decent amount of followers on Facebook, Twitter and any of the other big social media networking sites, you could increase your visibility faster than with any other means available today. It is so much easier than you would think to accomplish.

The best part: it is completely free! Joining these sites, building your profile and getting people to subscribe to you does not cost you a penny.

The key to your success on social media is to focus on providing value to your followers. Do not use it purely as a means to promote your business or you won't do very well. The best companies that use social media effectively do so by creating a community among their followers.

---

[4] http://expandedramblings.com/index.php/by-the-numbers-17-amazing-facebook-stats/

This includes polling them, getting to know their followers intimately, reaching out to them, providing valuable information completely free of charge and being contactable. Starting a conversation and really engaging with your followers is a sure fire way to success with your online social media campaigns.

You could also employ gamification tactics to make customer interactions more enjoyable. This is a rather new concept that only rose in popularity quite recently.

Gamification is basically turning the social engagement of your prospects into a game. You entice people to share your content on their social media profiles and to have other people gather likes and/or follows on the various social media sites, by asking their friends to join. You then reward them for helping you by offering discounts, prizes or free stuff. You could create challenges and a spirit of competition by adding multiple levels to the "game". For example: "For every 25 of your friends that you can convince to like my page, I'll offer you a 1-hour marketing consultation call for free." Wouldn't you try and get a few hundred people to like my page if I offered something like that? I know I would.

Answer the two most important questions

Why should they buy what you are offering?

And

Why should they buy what you are offering <u>from you</u>?

If you can properly answer these two questions and make that answer clear to potential prospects easily and very early on in the interaction, you increase your chances at being successful in your sales by many folds. In marketing terms, this is usually referred to as your unique selling proposition.

Most people tend to make emotional purchase decisions. They don't care as much about the features of the product as they care about the promised results that you can offer. They want to know that buying those pills are going to make them smarter or live a longer and more fulfilling life. They want to know that they are effective anti-aging pills, not that they contain resveratrol and turmeric root extract. Those pieces of information, although important, more often than not, don't help you sell the pills. It's the end, not the means, which market your product.

The second question is: why they should buy it from you? This is where you need to differentiate yourself from others who might be selling similar products or services. What sets you apart from the crowd? What makes you unique? What is your unique selling proposition (USP)? Could it be that you offer the best quality service to your customers? Could it be that you have a better quality product? Maybe your guarantee policy is better than your competitors. Once again, it's all about getting them to trust you.

Ultimately it all boils down to one thing. All it takes to build authority is to connect your list of prospects and customers with your know-how and your unique gifts.

CHAPTER 3

Designing the ideal product / service catalogue

You might already know what you are selling, but are you missing anything? This chapter is about creating the ideal product or service catalogue for your business.

If you are a business owner, your whole business is probably centred on a product or a service already. Yet, you are probably reading this book because you have a bigger vision for your business than the level reached.

I aim to refine your offer to the best of your business' capacity. Maybe, and just maybe, if you added or removed a few products or services from your total list of offerings, you would achieve that vision faster.

When I make a new sale, I don't really mind if my brand new customer only spends three dollars with me. My product offering is designed in such a way that I always have something else to offer after the initial sale. The best term for this concept is the Long Term Value of a Customer, or LTV.

Take John, for example. John was a prospect until he bought a three dollar e-book from my website about concept XYZ. In reading that e-book, he chose to build a website with my company's help. He then hired us to do some general marketing consulting to help him determine the best path to take moving forward in his business. John's long-term value as my customer was in fact thousands of dollars rather than just the initial three-dollar e-book that he originally bought. Nonetheless, if I didn't have that three-dollar e-book, he might have never become my customer.

What are some of the different types of sales?

In marketing, there is a concept called the Sales Funnel, or the Customer Flow Chart. This business marketing term defines the different possible paths that a customer can take whilst doing business with you.

There are different types of sales that you can make or offer to a customer, depending on the situation.

The most common type of sale is usually referred to as a direct sale. A direct sale takes place when a prospect wants to fulfil a specific need and you have the right product or service for that need. You directly offer them what they want and they buy it from you. The transaction ends and you have made your sale.

Another type of sale that might be familiar is usually referred to as an upsell. An upsell is usually done right before completing the transaction of a direct sale. While you are fulfilling a customer's need, you suggest a complementing product or service to the original sale. This is called an upsell and it's a fantastic way of adding additional revenue streams to your business. Once a potential customer has their credit card in hand and is ready to purchase, they have already made the mental decision that you were trustworthy and they are way more likely to buy something else from you at that moment. If you have nothing to offer them, then you are essentially missing out on a perfect extra revenue stream.

Next, we have the cross sell. Cross selling is giving your customers the opportunity to buy something else from you that doesn't necessarily have anything to do with the original purchase. A famous example of this strategy in use is Amazon.com. If you haven't purchased anything on their site before, I think you should. The experience of doing business with them is phenomenal in my opinion. Just before allowing you to complete your purchase, as well as all the way throughout your shopping experience, they show you items that other customers have purchased along with what you are about to buy. This is a great example of a cross sell.

The last type of sale worth mentioning is the down sell. This is an often forgotten concept in business. Most businesses have a single core product or service that they offer for a standard price point, determined at the time of the product creation and based on the perceived value of the offer. They don't think about the fact that some prospects might not want to do business with them at that price point. A down sell is when you offer the product at a lower price point to avoid losing the sale altogether. It represents a way that your customers can get started working with you for a smaller amount of money before they make the bigger purchase.

As an example of this in my business, I offer a complete done-for-you social media marketing solution. For some of my customers, depending on the type of work involved, the cost for this service can range from hundreds to thousands of dollars per month. I know that many small businesses cannot afford this type of hit on their monthly cash flow. Therefore, I prepared an online learning program that I can offer for a nominal one-time fee of a few hundred dollars, where they can learn how to do exactly what I do for my customers on a monthly basis. They can then take matters into their own hands, do their own social media marketing and save themselves thousands of dollars. The power of this lies with the fact that those customers will often eventually come back to me to purchase the done-for-you offer. When the strategies I gave them start working, their businesses will grow significantly. They will be able to afford my larger services and they will give the work to me anyway, so that they can focus on building other areas of their business.

Customer Flow / Sales Flow

Now that you know the different types of sales, it's time to create the ideal customer flow chart or sales flow diagram for your business.

There are many different ways to accomplish this; thus you can't create a wrong ideal customer flow or diagram.

Start by thinking about the various types of customers that do business with you. Do they typically have deep pockets? Maybe some of them are rather cheap. Are your customers more visually interactive or do they interact better to sound? Come up with a list of characteristics about their possible wants and desires. If you are having trouble with this task, then just ask them. Don't ever be ashamed to ask your existing customers how you can better serve them. It's part of your market research and it can prove to be invaluable to the way you ultimately build your business and to the profitability potential that you can achieve as a result.

Next, take your main product or service offering and work on identifying some possible upsells, cross sells and down sells. Once the list is created, organize this information onto a chart or a diagram in such a way that your customers can easily flow from one part of the diagram to the next.

Take a look at my customer flow diagram:

- $10 – E-book on business marketing
- $20 – "Build it and they won't come" book
- $197 – Webinar series covering most of the concepts of this book in more detail
- $1000 - $3000 small business marketing services
- $3000+ personal one-on-one marketing consultation

This diagram is designed in such a way that a typical prospect turned customer for a minuscule ten dollars can eventually make me thousands of dollars. This is my intention with each and every one of my customers. I am being incredibly transparent with you. My intention for you reading this book right now is for you to become my customer and do lots of business with me for a very long time. I know that some of you might not continue along the funnel, but that's why we call it a funnel. For those of you ready to take the next step, I know that I have the right service for you.

Types of Products or Services

Here are some ideas of products or services that you could add to your offerings catalogue in your business. This list is by no means exhaustive, but might spark some creativity in your mind, causing you to create the amazing catalogue that your business deserves.

E-Book	Book	CDs
DVDs	Webinar Series	Seminars
Newsletters	E-mail List	Private Groups
Masterminding	Personal Coaching	Group Coaching
1-on-1 Coaching	Membership Site	Online Course
In-Class Course	T-shirts	Mugs
Hats	Booklets	Workbooks
Pens		

As mentioned, there are other ideas and things that you can use to enhance your product offering. Start by looking at the previous list and see if anything sticks out at you. Could you take an idea such as a webinar series and mould it into something that would fit your business model? If so, then do it, and add it to your offering. Get people excited about what you do by involving them at different price points, so that you have something for everyone. If done properly, you will always have a path between one part of the sales funnel and another. Ideally, you want your customers to move around in your sales flow diagram from one place to another. That's when you will be making a lot more money from each customer and you can start tracking the long-term value of your average and ideal customers.

If you plan on having a good portion of your sales flow or your funnel available for purchase on your website, here are the ideal price ranges that I would suggest according to my personal experience.

Products for automated online sales should range between $27 dollars on the low end and a maximum of $500 on the high end. It's not always the case but typically, in offering products at less than $27, the cost of supporting those customers is higher than the profit that you end up making from the sale. Furthermore, items being sold online should not exceed $500 because typically most customers want to be reassured of your trustworthiness face to face or at least over the phone before committing to such a large purchase. These have been my findings and though they are not completely set in stone, they should serve as temporary guidelines. If you intend to offer certain items online that do not require your direct attention to fulfil, such as e-books or online courses, you should typically stick to those price ranges. I have gotten the best results using these numbers.

Repurposing Content

There is a great way of adding significantly more products to your overall offering without too much effort on your part. The concept is referred to as repurposing content.

Ultimately, the goal in repurposing content is taking the content you are already actively selling and improving sales by recreating the same content in a different format.

Human beings are diverse in physical appearance, personality and tastes, but also in their learning process. Each and every one of us has a more developed sense, which we rely on to efficiently absorb information. Some are visual learners; they love to watch videos in order to learn. Others prefer to read about a topic of their interest and others, still, are auditory learners; they prefer to listen to the content that they plan on learning.

With that in mind, how can you take great content and repurpose it, so as to offer it in more formats for different types of audiences?

What I did in my business was to take the content of this book and recreate it in webinar format. Visual learners can watch it on the Internet rather than reading the book in its physical form. I have also created an audio version of this book for those who assimilate more easily by listening to the content of this book rather than by reading it. This concept provides me with a wider range of customers that can access my information and thus, produces increased income.

Other examples of repurposing content include creating blog posts on a topic that was recently discussed or a question that you answered on your latest live webinar that you hosted. Perhaps you could take the book that you wrote, create a condensed version and sell it online as an e-book. You could also start a podcast or create a press release if you can manage to relate an event in your business to the local news. You can definitely come up with valuable content to share on your various social media profiles.

I hope that this chapter gave you plenty of ideas on how to improve your product or service offering. By following my advice, I know that you will achieve your goals much faster than originally anticipated.

CHAPTER 4

Why you need to bring your business online

There is no doubt in anybody's mind these days that having a website for your business builds credibility.

Nowadays, consumers are favouring Google search in finding a business over opening up the phone books. That is not surprising, considering that the Internet is usually a lot quicker and the information is usually more up to date than in other mediums.

With how easy it has become in recent years to start a website, business owners are also favouring the online existence over paying for a spot in the phone books. It is usually more economical for the entrepreneur and is much more effective, since the business owner can control what is displayed to the end user.

However, a lot of small business owners get scared by just starting to build their presence online.

Some fears that could be more prevalent amongst business owners are:

- It's going to cost too much
- I'm not technical enough
- It'll take way too much of my time to maintain

- I don't know where to start

I would like to take the opportunity to show you how affordable having your own website can be. In fact, you should be able to get your business online for as little as a few hundred dollars.

You don't need to know anything about building websites, HTML code, and other technicalities to get this going. New advancements in technology, including content management systems (CMS) such as the popular Wordpress platform, can help you build a professional looking website quickly and without needing any technical skills at all.

Contrary to popular belief, building your website is also not very time-consuming. There are literally hundreds of thousands of freely available website designs, themes and templates that you can easily download and use for your website. The only thing that can take you time is to gather the content that you want displayed on your site. All the rest can be done incredibly quickly and easily.

As far as knowing where to start, if you are reading this book and have made it this far in, then you are on the right path. My goal is to bring you all the information and knowledge you need in order to easily implement the discussed marketing strategies into your business, immediately after reading this book.

For those of you who feel inclined, I will be providing a way to get in touch with my company and me, so that we can help you succeed in implementing the techniques described in this book.

Having a site builds credibility

Without any doubt, having a website for your business builds instant credibility. It makes your business look professional and composed, while providing an easier alternative to finding information than picking up the phone. However, not all websites are created equally. A poorly designed website can in fact hurt your credibility and reputation.

Showcase your products / service

What better way to get people interested in purchasing what you have to offer than to have it portrayed on your very own website, along with all the benefits and features that they will obtain upon purchase?

Setting up the product or service for online sales is an efficient method of instantly attracting more business overall. Showcasing the product or service on the internet equals more sales.

Provide 24 / 7 Accessibility

Upon launching your website for the first time, all of a sudden you realize that your business is now open 24 hours per day and 7 days a week.

Your customers have access to see who you are and can get to know your business, not just when the physical storefront is open, but at their own convenience.

They can contact you by e-mail and even purchase products or services from you outside of your normal business hours.

Once your website is launched, you never have to lose another sale again by reason of your opening hours.

Deliver your message to a broad audience

As soon as your site goes online, you are no longer a small local business. You are now opened both nationally and internationally as well. In fact, your business just became global.

People from all over the world are now able to publicly see who you are and can choose to do business with you in some way, shape or form.

This doesn't mean that you need to service customers globally if you don't want to. You can always adopt policies that let others know you only serve within your country. Nonetheless, you now have the possibility of expanding globally with very little effort.

Easily brand your company

Having a website for your business provides you with one more tool to help brand your company effectively. In fact, in my opinion, a website is probably one of the easiest tools to use in creating an overall brand or look and feel for your company.

I believe this to be true because websites are flexible in terms of appearance. You can make them look exactly how you want them to look. You can have them match the design of your existing flyers and business cards, or match your overall business concept.

Websites are also very easily marketed. The fact that they are available online for the world to see makes them an easy tool for increasing visibility.

Having a website is more practical than handing out business cards, since the cards need to be handed out one by one, whereas with a website, one big advertising campaign can bring you thousands of prospects. It is much more efficient.

Other reasons to have a website

- Receive payments for your products or services
- Reduce customer service costs and provide 24/7 customer support
- Share important business information easily and effectively
- Build a community of customers or followers
- Gain valuable market research
- Build trust with your prospects
- Create a greater awareness about your business
- Advertise more cost effectively

There are many more reasons than I can list here to bring your business online in this day and age. If you really stop to think about what having a website can bring to your business, you wouldn't even consider not have having one.

Remember that your first website does not need to be costly, time-consuming or complicated to set up. It can be very basic, as long as it is appealing to the eye and informative. Just get started and get something up.

One of my mentors, Alex Mandossian always says: "Sloppy success is better than perfect mediocrity". With this quote in mind, start by getting your site online and working for your business, rather than waiting until its perfect or until you have enough time to finish it properly. The site will work for you while you will take care of other pressing matters.

CHAPTER 5

Building your website

One of the first things that people do when they need to reach a local company is to run to their computer (or smart phone) and key in the name of that company on Google or a similar search engine. I know I do. Gone are the days of the local phone book or yellow pages. People don't have time to read through those big heavy books anymore, not when they can get the same information from Google in a fraction of the time.

In my opinion, one of the most important aspects of building the presence of your business online is the contact page of your website. It's probably the most valuable content that you will place on your site.

You might be thinking at least one of the following:

- It's too much work to put up a webpage
- It's too complicated to put up a webpage
- It's too expensive to put up a webpage
- I don't have time to put up a webpage

In fact, it doesn't have to be as hard as you think. It doesn't have to cost you a lot and you will be able to do it without much work involved if you take advantage of these amazing tools and resources.

Now, you now know that you need to build a website, but how on earth do you get started?

Start with a plan.

A good site is a properly planned site

Here's the deal. Everyone should create a plan before building their website. But how do you build a plan if you don't have any experience building a site? The old catch 22.

The only prerequisite to building a proper web design plan is having been to a website before. I hope that everyone reading this book has at least been on the Internet before. You know what you like and what you don't like about websites. You know better than any web designer what sort of content your customers should see or read before making the decision to do business with you.

The overall idea with building the plan is to organize yourself so that you know what content you will be sharing and where the visitors will be able to find it on your website.

Start with a blank piece of paper and a pen. Draw a big rectangle and fill it in with the sections of your home page. Draw a nice big header section. You can put a sidebar on the left hand side of the page or the right hand side if you want a sidebar at all. Draw a space for the navigation bar, then start deciding what entries it will showcase. Determine how many pages long you initially want your website to be. This can always change to accommodate more or less pages.

The more you plan before you start, the easier it will be to implement the site later on.

I will now tell you some different things to take into consideration when designing your site. There are two significantly different ways to start. One is called building a brochure site and the other one is building a squeeze page site. However, you don't have to limit yourself to one. I will show you the differences in the next two sections.

If you're still not completely sure yet of what you want to accomplish with your site, **don't worry**. There is nothing stopping you from putting up just a simple one page website with your contact details. You owe it to your business to have that information up and accessible for your customers.

Brochure site and so much more

For most small businesses, having a small brochure site is a great starting place. This is what the vast majority of businesses will use to build their first site. Ultimately, a brochure site is like a business card on steroids.

It's primary purpose is to create awareness amongst your clients and prospects as to who you are, what you sell, where you are located, as well as your pricing and how to get in touch with you.

This is how the navigation bar would normally look:

Home	News	Products	About Us	Contact

This site wouldn't have too many features. Its goal would be to replace the phone book entry, let people know you exist and hopefully drive them to call you or visit your place of business. It generally consists of a few static pages, yet fulfills its purpose for most of them.

Once you build a brochure site, you can expand it much further. You can take it to the next level by including a shopping cart system that would allow your website visitors to purchase from you online or you could add photo galleries to your website. You could offer free gifts when your visitors leave you their e-mail addresses or you could integrate your social media profiles into the site. Your possibilities are almost endless.

To squeeze or not to squeeze

Another type of site that you can create is called a squeeze page. Most people would not consider this a complete site, given that is made of a single page. It also exists in the form of a combination of a squeeze page and a landing page, or a launch page.

Its purpose is very different than that of a typical website, since a squeeze page is designed primarily for lead capture.

You would create a single page with your logo; a header with a tagline, and the body of the site would contain some great content. Usually, you would place a few testimonials on the page. Some people like to place a video describing what they do. However, it is not mandatory, seeing that squeeze pages have proven to be very effective with or without a video on the page. It really depends on what message you are trying to convey.

The important factor in a squeeze page is that there are no links to any other part of the site or any other site on the Internet. The only action that a visitor should be able to make on your site is to submit their e-mail address to you.

Ideally, you would entice them to leave their e-mail address in exchange for something of value such as an e-book, a video series, or a webinar invitation. One of my favourite Internet marketers, Alex Mandossian, calls this: "ethical bribery".

The reason you would want a squeeze page is to collect their contact details so that you can build a powerful marketing platform.

How to start building your site

I promised that it wouldn't be complicated to create your own website so here's the secret; use a CMS platform. CMS stands for content management system which is a funky way of saying a point and click website creation platform that is really easy to learn and use.

The most commonly used and most well known platform these days is called Wordpress.

Wordpress is free to use and can be downloaded from www.wordpress.org. In order to use it, you would download the software and install it on a web hosting server. As complicated as that sounds, it really isn't. They have simplified the installation to what they call their "Famous 5-

minute installation". The following website will provide you with the installation steps:

http://builditandtheywontcome.com/wp-install

Once installed, your website will be up and running. Wordpress offers you what they call the admin dashboard, which is where you make all the changes to your site. There are hundreds of tutorials available for free on YouTube that explain how to use Wordpress in effectively building your website. It's very easy to learn, and with some tweaking on your own, you could probably figure it out for yourself.

There are other free CMS platforms available for use, but I prefer Wordpress. Here are my top 10 reasons for choosing Wordpress for all of my website needs:

1. Wordpress is a truly free and open source. Using their software on your website will never cost you anything. It is highly supported by a large community of developers.
2. You have the ability to update any content on your own without hiring a web designer. The user-friendly dashboard handles all the coding for you.
3. The visual editor and CMS features are unparalleled. It is easy to create new pages, add menu items, move things around, and include pictures and videos and so much more, just with the click of your mouse.
4. The are enough Plugins available for you to easily add features and extensions to your website. These extensions would otherwise cost thousands of dollars to implement from scratch.

5. There are libraries with literally hundreds of thousands of themes and website designs ready for use. No need to be graphically inclined. Just choose a design and enable it on your site.

6. Wordpress is already optimized to be very friendly to search engine bots, allowing your website to be found easier on the search engines.

7. It has easy integration with the most common social media networking sites. With the help of simple plugins, your Wordpress site can automatically post your new article to your Facebook fan page for example.

8. Wordpress is completely standards compliant, which means that your site will work on over 97% of the major web browsers, mobile browsers, search engines, screen readers and more.

9. You can rest assured that your website is secure and won't be hacked. The Wordpress community of developers are always releasing updates and security patches to prevent any security flaws.

10. And the best reason to use Wordpress is the ability to add a blog to your site. Most businesses have a blog, since it is a great way to provide valuable content to your customers and to position yourself as an authority in your niche.

Always have a blog

Most entrepreneurs make the mistake of not updating their site often enough. The simple and elegant solution to this issue is building a blog and writing posts or articles for the customers.

This is an easy way of giving your website visitors a reason to come back to your website more often.

It's also a great way to get recognized by search engines so that your website ranks well among other websites in your niche.

Having a blog doesn't necessarily mean that you need to spend hours every day writing long articles about your products or services. A blog post typically shouldn't exceed 3 to 4 short paragraphs. As long as you post a few times a month, you should do fairly well.

Of course, the more you post blog entries to your site, the more other websites will want to link back to you, which is a key strategy of popularizing your website and increasing traffic.

Where to host your site

What is hosting and why do you need it? Web hosting is basically renting space for your website on the Internet. You can build your website, but if you want to make it accessible, you need to place it on a physical server somewhere in the world. The actual location is not that important for the most part. That server is connected to the Internet and allows the rest of the world to visit your website.

Professional companies will take care of the server and web hosting management for you. They are called web hosting companies and most of them offer their services for a very affordable price.

Hostgator is one of the most well known hosting companies. They have large datacenters, with servers that have been tweaked and are known to work well with Wordpress. Here is their link for online hosting:

http://builditandtheywontcome.com/hosting

The two main packages that you should consider are the Hatchling or the Baby package. The only real difference between the two is whether you have one website address for your website or multiple addresses. If you choose to have multiple addresses, then you should purchase the Baby plan for a few extra dollars per month.

Using the coupon code *biatwc25pct* on the checkout page will get you an instant 25% off your entire order. Isn't that awesome?

What if you just don't want to do it?

If, at any time while reading this book, you consider that there is just too much information to handle, or you do not wish to handle the online marketing of your business, don't worry.

My company, Kwik-Web, offers one on one training programs to learn all of the concepts and techniques outlined in this book. During these training programs, we will show you how to not only build your website but also to maintain it and make changes on your own. We strongly believe that you shouldn't be tied to a Webmaster. You should learn to be your own web master.

We then take you by the hand and show you how to properly market your site, so that you can attract visitors, prospects and customers to your site. We can setup lead capture forms and a great e-mail marketing campaign platform for you as well.

If you don't like the "sit down and learn it" approach to your marketing, we also offer many done-for-you options. Our team of skilled marketers will work to build your online marketing platform for you, with little involvement on your part.

If you wish to learn more about the various options please visit us at:

http://builditandtheywontcome.com/kwik-web

As a reward for reading my first book, I want to extend a special offer to those visiting my website and wanting to work with Kwik-Web. Visit the site in order to find out what the special offer is.

CHAPTER 6

How to attract visitors and leads

It's one thing to build your website and a whole other thing to get people to visit. Referring back to the title of this book, remember that it's not good enough to just build your website. You need to actively market to attract visitors. Your website will only serve you if you can get people to view it.

First, I want to go over a few concepts, so that you better understand what I mean:

Generic Traffic vs. Targeted Traffic vs. Referral Traffic

Generic traffic can be defined as traffic that is completely unknown. The website does not have any information on the demographics or the psychographics of the visitors. It can be equated to leaving some flyers on the windshields of people's cars at a grocery store. You have no way of knowing who they are or what their likes and dislikes are.

Targeted traffic can be harder to obtain. It is basically traffic that comes to your site based on predetermined information. Targeted traffic comes in based on high-level information, such as age range or gender. It is also possible to target visitors based on really low-level or detailed measures, such as the type of movies they watch or their favourite colours.

Referral traffic, however, is a different story. It is traffic that is referred to your site by someone else or by another site. This can be very valuable because you can take advantage of the trust relationship that was already built with the visitor on the previous site.

Unqualified Prospect vs. Qualified Prospect

In order for visitors to be considered as prospects, they need to enter your sales funnel. This can be different for every sort of business and can be defined many different ways.

An unqualified prospect is someone who, like the generic traffic example, does not provide any information prior to or upon entering your site. He/she might be willing to buy from you, but you would have no way of knowing in advance.

A qualified prospect is someone who has gone through the qualification process. He meets many or most of the requirements defined in your niche statement. He came to your website looking to purchase what you sell and you just need to show him the way.

Buyer vs. Browser

There are two types of users on the Internet; there are buyers and there are browsers. Although one can become the other at different times, convincing them to change is hard work.

Buyers are people with a strong propensity to spend. They are online with the intention of finding what they are looking for and acquiring it.

Browsers, on the other hand, are using the Internet for one thing mainly: looking for information. They want to learn about something or find out the answer to a question. They are not necessarily looking to purchase anything. However, they can often be swayed to purchase something online.

Although we can place a lot of value on referral traffic, let's derive our success formula as follows:

Targeted traffic + Qualified prospects + Buyers = Big $$$

Great, now that we have an idea and know whom we are targeting, we can start looking into different ways of increasing your visibility online.

What is a lead?

A lead is a person who has been attracted by one or more of your advertisements or marketing methods. They proceeded to visit your website, browse around and executed at least one action which allows you to identify them. Until they perform an action and offer you their information, they are mere unqualified prospects.

In order for them to be considered a lead, you need to capture something from them, such as their name, phone number or e-mail address. You need to make sure that you have a way to follow up with them and convert them into a paying customer.

These types of actions include:

- Creating an account on your site

- Leaving a comment on your blog
- Signing up for your newsletter
- Purchasing something on your site
- Filling out a "contact us" form

Once they've done any of the actions above, they are considered a lead, because you now have something precious of theirs: their contact details. You can thus follow up with them as you please.

Where can you get them?

There are tons of ways to attract people to your website. However, keep in mind that attracting generic traffic is not good enough.

For the sake of clarity, I shall split the ways of attracting leads into two different categories: the ones attracted by online marketing methods and the ones attracted using offline, traditional marketing methods. In either case, the objective is the same. You want to pique their interest, so that they are ready and willing to hear more about what you have to offer.

I will list a few methods of sparking interest and will go over some of them in greater detail further in the book.

Online Marketing Methods

- **Social Media Marketing** – This is a great way to create a community with your prospects. It shows that there is a real person behind your business. It offers your customers an easy way to get in touch with you. This strategy doesn't have to cost you anything to implement and is hugely effective.

- **E-mail List Marketing** – A very popular way to provide a lot of value to your customers and to offer them a way to take action. This can be set up for a very inexpensive monthly rate. However, it is only as effective as the quality of the e-mails that you send out.

- **Pay Per Click Advertising** – This is a tricky one; I have seen it work wonders for some businesses and do a terrible job for others. It can be effective at almost any budget level, but its success depends on the keyword phrases that you choose to display your ads for.

- **Pay Per Impression Advertising** – This method works very well for building a brand, but can get expensive quickly if not controlled properly.

- **Search Engine Marketing** – This can either cost you a lot, or not cost you anything depending on how you implement it. Either way, it is a must for your business. If you do this effectively, you will increase your visibility in organic search results.

- **Online Press Release Submission** – There are many small online news websites are willing to publish your release just to fill their content quotas. This can be a huge boost of visibility with little effort on your part; you only need to write an article and send it off. There are free ways of sending your release to hundreds of sites.

- **Social Bookmarking** – This is a very popular free service that lets the world know what you're reading or what you like on the Internet.

- **Blogging** – Blogging is a great way of getting your website visitors to keep coming back for more great content. If you have good articles, people will read them and once they are there you can get them to take action.

Offline Marketing Methods

- **Press Release Submission** – Offline press releases, while effective, can prove to be costly. If you have something to share that is newsworthy, then it's in your best interest to submit it to the news agencies.

- **SMS Marketing** – Probably one of my new favourite offline marketing methods. This concept is fairly new. You build a list of cell phone numbers and then you send them SMS messages marketing your product or service. The open rate on an SMS is more than 98%[5] and it doesn't cost very much at all.

- **Printed Advertisements** – Depending on your business, this can be very effective and in some cases, not at all effective. If you have a local business and print flyers, distributing them should get you somewhere between a 6% to a 10% response rate.

- **Business Cards** – These little tools can be far more effective than how they are usually used. I will share with you an amazing strategy for business cards later on in the

---

[5] http://www.practicalecommerce.com/articles/4139-Text-Messaging-Effective-for-Retailers-

book. I will also offer you a way to get them printed very inexpensively.

- **Newspaper** – While it is a very old-school method for marketing, most people would agree that it isn't very effective anymore. Nowadays, more and more people tend to read their news online. Newspapers are still charging very high rates for printed ads.

- **Radio Ads** – This can still be effective for some businesses, but expensive overall. Radio usually works better for local businesses and only with a radio spot during any drive time. Outside of drive time your radio spot can be useless in most cases.

- **Event Promotion** – Promoting your business at someone else's event is a huge way to market your business. You are basically using the trust relationship that has already been built up between the event promoter and the group of people attending to boost your chances of success.

- **Billboards** – Also a very old-school method. I personally don't look at billboards anymore or pay very close attention to them. I'm sure some people do, but once again, unless your billboard is in a prime location I wouldn't count on this being your big ticket to lots of web traffic.

It is essential to know how to attract good quality leads, because these will eventually turn out to be your customers. The better leads that you collect, the better customers you ultimately have.

Grabbing their information

You've marketed your website through the various online and offline marketing methods previously outlined. Now, let me show you how to keep visitors on your website, before giving you tips on how to get back in touch with them.

Lure visitors in with witty, funny or interesting content. Make it your best content and don't charge for your best stuff. Give away free content and use that as bait for e-mail addresses gathering. You can write a short book or an e-book and offer it for free in exchange for an e-mail address. Studies have shown that having a good e-book with valuable content is one of the most effective and proven ways to convince someone to opt-in to your mailing list. You do not need to be the person who writes it. In fact, this is a good opportunity to create a mini joint venture with someone who has written an e-book and who will let you share the resulting list of e-mails. Using someone else's content can save you a lot of time and hard work. Just make sure that you have the right to freely distribute the e-book, so you don't infringe on any copyrights and that you don't alter the material in any way without the original author's prior consent.

Another way you can get them to leave their information is to offer them an outrageous and irresistible free gift.

If you can, stay away from the word "free" and use "complimentary" instead. I have found that using the word "free" tends to discount the value of what you are offering.

On the other hand, people love to receive gifts, especially when they are free.

Offer to send them something in the mail in exchange for a few dollars in shipping and handling. If you don't want to deal with shipping, then make something available for immediate digital download.

For example, you can offer an e-book or a video series where they can learn more. You can invite people to attend a webinar. You can offer them a 1-on-1 coaching session over Skype. You could even offer some coupons that they can use by visiting your store.

By the way, you never have to deal with shipping and handling if you don't want to. Just do a quick Google search for fulfillment houses and you can find lots of different companies that will take on that task on your behalf. It is becoming more affordable than you would imagine.

A great resource for this is Amazon.com. Since building some of the biggest warehouses and most efficient systems in the world, they have decided to branch out from just a simple online book store and now they rent out their warehouse space and fulfillment services for great prices. Check them out and see for yourself how easy it can be to start shipping out a physical product to your customers.

It is a lot easier and timely to offer something in a digital format rather than a physical one. Such as PDFs, e-books, audio clips, videos, newsletters, etc. However, offering something physical provides you with more information from the visitors, such as their mailing address, which grants you one more opportunity to market further.

Offering something physical is also great because you can collect shipping and handling fees. Now, the minute someone takes out their credit card and types it in to buy something from you, they are automatically much more likely to use it again. You have just created a trust relationship between you and your prospect. A prospect that has paid you anything is now considered a customer, even if it's only for a free gift that they just had to pay shipping.

When you craft e-mail messages to be sent to your list, try to inspire or evoke emotion in the way that you write your copy. Emotion moves people towards action and action is exactly what you want. Make sure that your e-mail copy is congruent with what is on your website. Make sure that it has been articulated clearly and that it's easy to understand. Put a lot of effort into crafting your subject line, because it determines if your readers will actually open your e-mail or not.

The next thing you should have on your website is a properly crafted sales page, that inspires visitors to take action when they get there. Speak to their fears and what they stand to gain. Make sure that your sales page has the following components:

Introduction – Introduce who you are and why you are writing to the audience today.

Problem Statement – Let them know that you feel their pain and understand them.

Agitate the Problem – Write it in a way to make them really feel the pain of their problem and push just enough to ensure it hurts.

Provide a Solution – You have a solution and are willing to provide it to them for a small fee.

Why you created the product – They need to know your intentions. Why do you want to help them and why did you create the solution?

Product Features in bullets – Don't go into too much detail about features. Customers buy results, not features.

Provide the results and benefits – Here is where you go into much more detail. What are the results that they will receive or achieve if they purchase your offer?

Offer bonus items – Always provide as much value as you can possibly provide. Give away incentives to entice people to purchase from you.

Iron clad guarantee – Reverse the risk by providing a guarantee that they can't refuse.

Order area – Probably the most important part of the page, because this is where you make the money.

Testimonials – Let the prospects know what other customers thought about your offer and how they benefited from it.

Something else that you can offer would be an x-part mini course or webinar series in exchange for their contact details. This can be very effective and it allows you to provide another chance to really show your visitors that you can offer them significant value. The easiest way to start building and delivering a mini course like this is to sign up for an e-mail contact manager service that supports an auto-responder feature.

If you have some form of service that requires a regular membership, then you can offer a trial membership for a specific time period. This is a great way for your prospects to see what you offer and how beneficial it can be for them. If you are going to offer a trial membership, try and offer a full service membership. If you offer limited content for the free trial, people often won't stay interested. You want to be able to give them the best chance to use or try out your service to convince them to pay you for it.

There should really only be two options for visitors of your site. They should be able to either A) buy something or B) leave you their e-mail address. If they come to your website, get what they need and leave before doing one of the two things I just listed then you are not serving them properly and, you are doing your business an injustice.

A few more great ways to collect leads on your website that I won't go into too much detail on right now are the following:

Squeeze Pages - These are web pages with the sole purpose of capturing a lead of a visitor by providing some content in exchange. It will be the vehicle to deliver your e-book or other digital content.

Contests - A great way to get some leads is to offer a contest where contestants can have the possibility of winning a prize of some sort.

SMS Marketing - One of the marketing strategies with the highest penetration rate. SMS messages have over a 97% open rate, which makes it very effective to deliver marketing messages. You can offer something in exchange for visitors enrolling in your SMS list.

QR Codes - These fancy new square codes are a fun way to get people with smartphones to join your lists. These QR codes are popping up everywhere and you can have your QR code send the prospect to a simple signup form.

I've covered a lot of different ways in this chapter to get new customers to your online storefront. In the next few chapters, I will go into much more detail on how to use these specific methods to attract more leads the right way.

CHAPTER 7

Social Media Marketing

Social media marketing is a form of online marketing that utilizes the common social media networking sites such as Facebook, Twitter and Pinterest, as well as others, to promote brand exposure and customer reach.

The main goal of a good social media marketer is producing content that the followers of the site find valuable enough to share among their followers or friends. This allows your message to reach a much broader audience very quickly and can help you build your brand for your business.

To be effective in social media marketing (SMM) you don't necessarily need to hire a professional SMM company to take over your online profiles. You can do this yourself in as little as 30 minutes per day. It takes some work to get it all started, but if you follow the tips in this chapter, you should be fairly well off. Of course, if at any point you decide that you don't want to do this yourself, my company also offers SMM packages that are done-for-you. We can create the profiles for you, set them up completely, get you started with a base of followers or friends, and then either let you maintain it on your own or we can offer you a monthly maintenance contract.

For further details, you can visit:

http://builditandtheywontcome.com/SMM

There are many pitfalls and mistakes that you can make with social media marketing. Therefore, I will be focusing on what to avoid before embarking on your first social media journey. Remember that you are playing with your reputation online. Just like in real life, your reputation online can take months to build up and just minutes to destroy.

Common pitfalls with social media marketing

Social media is a powerful tool if used properly. It is a second opportunity to create a real reputation, almost like in high school. Here are the 5 fastest ways to absolutely destroy any reputation that you will have or could have built up using social media.

This applies to your personal profiles and pages on all social media platforms for which you have an account, as well as any business related fan pages or profiles. It is important to realize that your customers or prospects will find you even if you differentiate your personal profile from your business profile.

Pitfall #1 Crazy self-promotion

- One of the big mistakes that many people make is spending too much of their time talking about their accomplishments or how good they are at their job and/or business. As much as it's entertaining, it is important to realize that all this is accomplishing is to play big on your ego and is not directly benefiting your customers in any way. Self-promotion is important to a point, but be very careful how much of it you do and how it will appear to others. Never bash another person or another company in order to promote yourself.

Pitfall #2 Pouring out your problems

- Another mistake that a lot of people tend to make is to spend a lot of time talking about the things that they have trouble with or don't do well. That's not always a bad idea, because social media is an amazing source to get help from the general crowd in finding solutions to the most challenging problems. The important thing to keep in mind is to not always use this as a vehicle for solving your troubles. It's important to use alternative methods to solving your problems as well. If you focus on solving them all via social media marketing, you may lose credibility. It doesn't look good if you constantly need the help of others to run your affairs.

Pitfall #3 Not controlling your privacy settings

- Most people don't even know how to control their privacy on social media. With some of the recent changes that have been happening with Facebook, Twitter, Google+ and others, it is so much easier to have fine-grained control over who gets to see certain content on your profiles. You can usually create groups of friends or contacts, and only display certain posts to one group versus another. If used properly, you can safely release the pictures of your drunken stupor to your friends from the night before without needing to worry about the coworkers in your office seeing them the next morning. Also, you need to watch out for whom you allow to post content on your profile. One of the fastest ways to ruin your reputation on social media is to allow anyone and everyone to post pictures to your Facebook timeline. Imagine how fast you would lose a business deal if the other party looked at your timeline, or got a notification in their newsfeed, and they saw you tagged in a picture, passed out drunk from the night before on your friends couch!

Pitfall #4 Completely automating your posts

- Another mistake that a lot of companies make is automating the release of all of their social media posts. There are services popping up each and every day, allowing you to automate the release of material to your social media profiles and pages. This is a great advantage to busy business individuals who don't have the luxury of time to connect every couple of hours to update their social media. The problem with this is that you are being fake. People see quickly through the facade. If you want to be effective, you need to create a conversation and build a community through authenticity. You can't expect to be successful by posting random quotes and information about your products.

Pitfall #5 Never having a conversation

- Last but not least, we have the lack of information in the form of a conversation on social media pages. The only, I repeat, the ONLY way to be successful on social media is to engage with your friends, fans, followers, etc... If you don't engage and converse with them, you are essentially alienating them and pushing them away. You need to talk to them, answer their questions, attend to their concerns, ask questions or poll them regularly. Share your concerns or thoughts on a matter, encourage them, make them laugh, etc.

I promise that if you avoid the five mistakes outlined above, you will be more successful on your social media campaigns than most businesses. There are still many other ways in which you can hurt your own reputation, but I believe that the five mentioned above represent the fastest way to do it. Avoid them, get engaged or involved in your social media campaign, and you are sure to succeed.

Setting up your social media profiles

Setting up your social media profiles is quick and easy. First, let me give you a short list of the social media websites that you should have accounts on:

- Facebook
- Twitter
- Google+
- Pinterest
- YouTube

There are tons of other social media sites, but I think these represent a good start for your marketing needs. You can always add more sites later on. If you do too much all at once, you will not be effective with any of them.

All of the social media websites above are completely free to join, to create accounts on and to post on.

Once the accounts are created, you will need to fill in your profile. Remember: with social media marketing, you are trying to build rapport with potential prospects and existing customers. If you create your profile page and leave most of it blank, they will probably think you are trying to hide something from them. Fill it in to the best of your ability and make it real. Don't lie on your profile in order to get it filled out; people will find out and that is a really fast way to lose followers and friends.

The next step is to upload your logo and cover image in the case of Facebook or logo and background image in the case of Twitter. If you already have something that you can use then it's really easy to set up. Just find the upload image button on the profile setup page and find the pictures on your computer. More than likely however you will need to make some adjustments to the size of the picture that you are using or it won't look very good.

If you don't have a logo, a background image or a cover image, then you can hire a professional graphic designer to make them for you. 99 Design is a really great site on which you can get in touch with graphic designers. On this site, graphic designers will create many different designs for you based on your product or service. Only when you find one that you like do you pay them for their work. By going to the following link, you will be redirected to the site:

http://builditandtheywontcome.com/99designs

The only thing left to do is to start posting. There are many things that you can post about. When writing a post for social media, always ask yourself the following question: how can I add more value to this post?

If you keep that in mind at all times, you will surely be successful in your social media marketing campaign.

What to post and how often to do it

The secret key to being successful with your social media campaign is to be real and to add value for your followers. If the content you post is "crapola" (as I believe the technical term is), people won't read it. If the content is full of useful information, then people will flock towards your page.

One of the main problems that business owners have is that they lack the understanding of the point of social media. The platforms were never meant to be used purely as a business marketing tool. They were designed to create social engagement between people. Not between brands/businesses and people but from one person to the next.

Therefore, you need to be real. Don't just post the latest article you wrote and hope that your fans will click the link and read it. Provide a voice for your business. Engage with your customers or prospects. Ask them questions or poll them on some topic. Get to know their likes and dislikes.

Learn something about each and every one of them and show them that you went through the trouble of doing so. Prove to them that you care about them and they will surely buy from you.

Giving free product is always an easy way to win over a crowd. Make it a game and make it fun and compelling. For example:

"For each of you who can convince 10 of your friends to like my Facebook Fan Page, I will personally send you an autographed copy of XYZ magazine featuring ABC completely free of charge a value of

Don't forget to give the value for a free give-away, especially if it is being given away in the context of a contest or a game.

My absolute best advice to you is to have fun with it. When it starts to feel like work, change something to keep it fun. The more fun you are having engaging with your customers, the more that fun will rub off on them. Once that happens, you've created a dedicated customer for life.

What else should you know?

Another thing you should do after generating followers on your social media profiles is using other resources on the Internet to drive more traffic towards your social media marketing campaigns.

You can accomplish this by adding social media links to existing content on your website or blog. You can change your e-mail signature to include links to your social media profiles, place the links on your business cards, etc.

You can also consider using Facebook ads as a new tool to drive significantly more traffic towards your page. This tool alone can make for a chapter. I will cover it in greater detail along with the pay-per-click advertising chapter.

CHAPTER 8

E-mail List Marketing

E-mail marketing is still one of the most effective online marketing methods available. It is easy to set up and is fairly inexpensive to implement.

E-mail list marketing is a form of marketing where you build a list of e-mail addresses from various sources and then proceed in sending them solicited e-mails on a regular basis to provide value and to promote your products or services.

Here's a little history lesson: in 2003 George W. Bush passed a law called the CAN-SPAM act, which set forth some strict rules about how commercial e-mail marketing should be handled online.[6] These rules made sure that members of the e-mail list could unsubscribe whenever they pleased. They also forced businesses to place a physical address at the bottom of every e-mail that they sent out. Of course, there are other rules to follow so that your e-mail is not considered as spam. The good news is that with most e-mail contact manager services you subscribe to online, you don't really need to worry about those rules, since they enforce them

---

[6] http://en.wikipedia.org/wiki/CAN-SPAM_Act_of_2003

automatically on your behalf before they allow you to send out an e-mail through their service.

Choosing an e-mail contact manager service

My first recommendation would be to find a good provider for the e-mail contact manager service. The more well known ones include:

- Aweber
- Constant Contact
- iContact
- MailChimp

There are also plenty of other providers that you can choose from, but I would suggest that you stick to the list above. Since their prices are fairly similar, let me go through the differences between them.

To start with, MailChimp offers a free tier option for those beginning on building their e-mail list. The thing to watch out for is that not all the options are included in the free package, yet their pricing for the paid tiers are still some of the best in the industry. They are constantly working on improving their rich visual editor for e-mails.

Aweber and iContact are fairly similar in terms of pricing and feature sets. They are both more advanced than MailChimp, but come at a greater monthly cost. In my opinion, Aweber is easier to use than iContact, while both of them offer fantastic services.

Constant Contact is my least favourite, but still quite useful and good. Their pricing is reasonable and their feature set is extensive. They even offer the ability to place video links, audio links and surveys directly in the e-mails. In my opinion, their interface takes longer to get used to, but once you figure it out, they offer a great service.

It's important to think about your decision and to choose the right service provider for your needs. Don't just read this sub-chapter and make your choice. Go on their websites and look up the real differences between them. Make an informed choice, because once you start building your list of e-mails, going back and changing your e-mail contact management service is a hassle.

How to build your list

Now that you have chosen your e-mail contact management service and set it up, you need to start building your e-mail marketing list. It wouldn't be too beneficial to send out e-mails without the actual addresses because they aren't going to reach anyone.

There are several ways to build your list effectively. We are going to go over a few ways that you can get people fairly quickly onto your list.

The first one that I will mention is placing a capture form on your own website. This is probably the most common method. It involves setting up a simple form where visitors to your website would enter their name and e-mail address and sign up on the spot to your list.

If you followed my advice earlier in the book and built your website using Wordpress, it can be as simple as installing a small plugin to your website and configuring it with the username and password that you setup with the e-mail contact manager. If your website is not built on the Wordpress platform, then it is usually as simple as copying and pasting basic HTML code onto your web page.

You can offer some form of incentive to get visitors to sign up to your e-mail list. This can be something like an e-book that you write or source from somewhere else. Maybe you can offer them a free consultation if you are in a service-based business. Another common offer is to invite people to watch a free webinar on your topic in exchange for them leaving you their e-mail.

Another great way to get people onto your e-mail marketing list is to use the power of social media. On Facebook, you can install an application onto your business Facebook Fan Page. This will allow visitors of your Fan Page to sign up directly to your e-mail list. You can also tweet or post links to a registration page. Once again, it's easier to fill your list if you incite people to join by offering them something for free.

One of my favourite methods of filling the list is simply asking people if they want to join, which they are willing to do most of the time. When I go to networking events and people offer me their business cards, I always ask if they would allow me to add them to my e-mail list. If you have a physical storefront or a restaurant or office space, you can offer the actual visitors something for free in exchange of leaving their e-mail address. For example, you can offer a free desert at a restaurant in exchange for an e-mail address.

What to write in your e-mails

I, like many other modern consumers, prefer text over embellished and colourful HTML based e-mails, simply because I prefer to read e-mails on my mobile phone. Even though most smartphones are capable of displaying rich full HTML e-mails, they take longer to load and in my opinion are harder to read. The modern consumer doesn't have the luxury of time. With text-based e-mails, one can easily scan through the text quickly and get the gist of the e-mail before choosing to read it or throwing it out.

As stated many times already throughout this book, just focus on providing value in your e-mails. Offer advice or tips to your subscribers. Give them information about your company or your industry that they can use and will want to read. Then, and only after you have provided them with useful information, offer them a call to action.

Make sure that there is only one call to action in your e-mail. If you offer too many choices, people won't know what to do and you will end up hurting your marketing efforts.

Your call to action can be as simple as asking them to like your Facebook Fan Page or to follow you on Twitter. You can ask them to give you a call if they wish to learn more about your products or ask them to visit a link to your website or product page, where you can market to them further.

CHAPTER 9

Pay Per Click Advertising

Pay per click is a form of advertising, actually first started by Google in 2002. This was their way of differentiating themselves from the other search engines, including Yahoo, who at the time was the biggest and most used search engine on the Internet. It was a way to bring relevant paid or sponsored search results to the top of the search engine results page.

The concept was very simple in the early years. A company would setup their advertised search listing and bid on some keywords that might be typed into the Google search box. When a user typed those search keywords the advertisers listing would show up first on the results page. If the end user clicked on that listing, then the advertiser would pay Google the amount that was bid for the click.

In recent years however, pay per click advertising has grown, along with other forms of online marketing. Now, there are literally hundreds of various ensembles offering some form of pay per click advertising. It is no longer restricted to a few sponsored results on the top of Google's search engine results page. You can find pay per click ads on the top of Google results, on the right hand side of the results list and on other search engines on the Internet. You can also find pay per click advertising on millions of independent websites throughout the Internet using Google's AdSense platform or other similar services from competitors. You can even find pay per click advertising on your favourite social media networks, such as Facebook. For the sake of simplicity however, I will only write about Google AdWords and Facebook Ads in this book.

Pay per click advertising can be a very lucrative and a very successful way for you to get more traffic to your website. However it can also cost you a lot of money and produce very little results if your campaign is not handled or managed correctly. Luckily, I aim to give you the necessary guidelines to be successful with your pay per click advertising campaigns. Let's get started by going over how to effectively research what keywords to bid on.

How to choose the best keywords

Choosing the right keywords to market your business or website can be challenging, as it requires creativity and patience to do it effectively. The good news is that you have access to a phenomenal tool, one that Google has spent a lot of time and money and time on building: the Google Keyword Research Tool. It has become the standard in performing keyword research. You can find it by going to the following URL:

http://builditandtheywontcome.com/keywords

The best way to start is to grab a pen and paper, then navigate to your own website. Go through all of the pages of your website one by one and start building a list on that paper you should have in front of you with all the different themes that you find. Look for keywords that describe the content on that page.

When I mention keywords, I am also including keyword phrases. This means that they can be anywhere from one to five words long. One and two word keyword phrases are usually referred to as short tale keywords and keyword phrases between three and five words long are usually referred to as long tale keywords.

Here are some examples of the types of keyword phrases:

> Back exercises for elderly women
> Raw vegan blueberry pie recipe
> Outside the box marketing tips for small businesses

Once you have a list, flip to the next page of your notepad and start a second one. The following list requires a little bit of creativity and thinking so get comfortable.

You will now brainstorm on the keyword phrases that you would like to be listed for on Google, but haven't yet found in your website. Think about your customers and prospects, and then determine what types of phrases they might type into Google or another search engine in order to find your website or business. Maybe you are already listed on the search engines for that term and maybe you aren't but would like to be. Write down as many as you can think of. Don't worry if you get stuck and cannot think of any more, the Google Keyword Research tool will help once you have finished creating your list. It will suggest other keyword phrases related to your list.

Great, now you have those two lists. The next step is going to the Google Keyword Research Tool. If you need that link again it is:

http://builditandtheywontcome.com/keywords

Once you are on that page, the only option that you need to change from the default option is to set it to "Exact Match" searches.

There are two really important numbers to look for: the number of global monthly searches (which should be greater than 2500 searches per month) and the estimated search results (which should be less than 250,000).

The number 2500 tests if the market exists and if enough people are looking for that keyword phrase. The number 250,000 tests the amount of competition that you will have in getting visitors to find your site with the corresponding keyword phrases.

Those numbers are not set in stone, but based on all of my testing and tracking; these numbers seem to work best. By all means, once you feel more comfortable with pay per click advertising, feel free to try out other forms of keyword vetting. Try different numbering combinations and seeing how they affect the performance of your campaign. However, if this were your first time, it would be in your interest to stick to the numbers that I have provided.

Here are the steps in verifying the strength of every keyword phrase you find.

Start with the very first keyword on your list and do the following steps for each keyword, one by one.

1. Enter the keyword or keyword phrase into the search box and then click search.

2. Take down the number for Global Monthly Searches and ensure that it is at least 2500.

3. If it is less than 2500, discard the keyword phrase. Before you do, check the list of suggested keywords from Google. If there are any that meet the 2500 Global Monthly Searches, mark them down.

4. Type the keyword or keyword phrase into a normal Google.com search box and click the search button.

5. Check the number of estimated search results, (which should be displayed right at the top of the search engine results page, just under the search box).

6. If the number of estimated search results is less than 250,000 results, then mark that keyword phrase down on a new list. If the number of search results is more than 250,000 results, you can cross out that keyword phrase and go onto the next one on your list.

Go back through the six steps above for each and every keyword phrase from your original two lists, as well as any of the keyword phrases that Google has suggested to you that met the 2500 global monthly searches test.

Once you have the final list of keyword phrases, you are ready to create the ad campaign for your site.

Creating your Ad Campaign

There are two different types of ad campaigns that can be run on the majority of pay per click advertising providers. You can create text-based advertisements or picture banner based advertisements.

In the case of picture banner advertisements, the ad provider will define the size requirements. In this case, either Google or Facebook. Google has all sorts of different sizes that they support on their platform. You should try and create the same ad campaign for as many different sizes as you can. To create the banner, you will either have to create it on your own using graphic editing software, or you can hire out that work to a graphic designer. Once again, a resource that I have already provided before but is worth mentioning again is 99 Designs. This is a site where you post what you are looking for and lots of graphic designers do the work. You get to choose from the finalized work that is provided to you and you only pay if you choose to use work from a designer on that site. The website can be found here:

http://builditandtheywontcome.com/99designs

As far as the content goes for the picture banner, try and keep the text short and sweet. It should be striking and catchy. It should inspire the browsers that find your ad to click it. Be careful however and make sure to keep it relevant to what the resulting website is about. If not, you will get unqualified leads which are people who click who are not really interested in what you are offering and will be paying clicks for nothing.

Text based advertisements are not all that different from the picture   banner ones, except that you won't need the help of a graphic designer to make it. It's all about how well you can write your marketing copy for your ads. My advice is pretty straight forward; once again, keep it catchy and striking. It should have a call to action embedded in the text. Remember that you only have three lines of four or five words to work with so keep it short and sweet.

The best thing to do is to try both the text and the picture banner ad for a few days and monitor the results through the platform that you are using. If you aren't getting any results or the results are not great, tweak the wording a bit and try it again. As long as you did the keyword research part properly, you should get some pretty good results after a little bit of tweaking in the wording. I call this concept "test, track, and tweak". Apply this over and over again until you are successful.

Targeting your Ad Campaign

The last step in an effective pay per click advertising campaign is to target your ads, so that they can be as effective as possible for your marketing efforts. Both Google AdWords and Facebook ads have very extensive targeting mechanisms, for which I will give you the basics, so that you can get started immediately. It would take me forever to go through all of the various ways for you to target your ads but the ones that I will write about here should be enough to get you started and on the right track.

First, you should think about your niche or market. As stated in the chapter on defining your niche, you can't be effective trying to sell to everyone in the world and if you still don't believe me on this point, go back and re-read the chapter on defining your niche. It's one of the most important concepts in this book.

Your niche is split up into demographics and psychographics. Believe it or not and as scary as it sounds, both Google and Facebook have most of this information about you and I already, as well as most people who use their services. Fortunately, you can use these data points as targeting methods for your advertisements.

Set up your advertisements so that only people who fit the definition of your ideal customer get to see them. You will pay much less in advertising costs and will get more qualified leads clicking your ads.

Do you only sell your product or service in one city, state, or country? If so, make sure to limit your advertisements location base parameters to the geographic locations that you serve. One of the last things that you want is for someone in Europe to be clicking your ad while you are paying for that click, only for them to find out that they can't even buy your product from your website because you only ship within North America.

The smaller your market is and the more targeted your ad is, the less you will pay per click, since you won't be competing against so many other businesses. Marketing is much easier if you position yourself as the leader of a niche. You want to be the big fish in the small pond as the cliché goes.

Lastly, I will mention the bid amount for each advertisement campaign. Both Google and Facebook will offer you a suggestion for the bid amount, which will usually range from a low to a high price. If you bid too low, then your advertisement might never be shown. If you bid too high, then you are just wasting your money. My best suggestion would be to take the high end suggested and lower it by about 10%. This should be your bid. That way, your listing will almost always be displayed and it will usually be one of the top 3 in the listing results. Don't be afraid to bid high on the per click price. If you followed my advice and your keywords are relevant, your advertisement is good quality, is catchy or inspiring and has the right call to action with defined targeting criteria, then you shouldn't mind paying a lot for attracting qualified leads. These are the ones who will most likely buy from you and who can become your best customers.

CHAPTER 10

Back Link Marketing Strategy

Let me start by defining what a back link is so you can better understand this chapter. A back link is a link on someone else's website that points back either to your home page or to another page on your website. For example, if you convince your product supplier to place a link on their website to your website, letting their visitors know where they can purchase those products, this would count as a back link for you.

Back links can be incredibly valuable for your website and it's important to know why. Search engines such as Google and Yahoo count back links as a kind of vote for your website. The more votes you get, the more credible your website is. The more credibility you have, the higher they will list your website in their search engine results page.

Another important factor is not just the quantity of back links that you have but also the quality of back links. Having thousands of back links pointing to your website from really low quality websites won't be worth nearly as much as having a few back links from high quality websites. The quality of a website is determined by thousands of data points, such as how relevant the content is, how many quality back links point to their website, how many visitors they get on a regular basis, how long the website has existed, the search keywords density, etc. Fortunately, you don't need to track any of these on your own, since Google has done a good job at creating a score for websites, called Google PageRank. PageRank is a score from one to ten that Google assigns to indicate the relevancy of a web page. A website with a PageRank of zero has absolutely no relevancy and a website with a PageRank of ten is considered a high quality web page.

Your goal with back link marketing is to find several high PageRank web pages that are willing to place a link on their site pointing back to you. This will give your website significant credibility and will help you improve your search engine rankings, thus making you much more visible to potential prospects. With more visibility, you will have more traffic to your website.

Common Pitfalls of Back Link Marketing

People often hurt their own reputation unintentionally by making some big mistakes when it comes to creating back links. Their intentions are genuine, but they don't implement the strategies properly and they end up with low rankings in the search engines.

It's a lot easier to build a site with good rankings if it hasn't already acquired a bad reputation than rebuilding good rankings on a site that has made significant mistakes. Bad decisions in regards to back link building are hard to recover from.

Pitfall #1

The first pitfall is having a link placed on a site that already has a very bad reputation. In most cases, it can actually harm your chances at having a good ranking. This includes sites that are SPAM or sites with duplicate content, such as replicated websites, porn websites or gambling websites.

Pitfall #2

Second, we have link buying or selling. Link buying is paying someone else who owns a website to place your link on theirs. Link selling would be charging someone else to place a link on your website. Most people make this mistake when they start. It's a lot easier to buy your way onto a website, rather than acquiring the necessary rankings with time. However, the search engines tend to frown on this. Doing it might even get you banned completely from some search engines.

Pitfall #3

Third, we have what is referred to as No Follow links. These are links on a specific website that are marked with some code behind the scenes letting the search engines know not to follow that link. Although this won't damage your reputation with search engines, it certainly won't do anything to help you out.

Pitfall #4

The next pitfall is getting back links from high PageRank sites that are in a completely different niche than yours. This doesn't really help you and should basically be avoided. If the site linking to you is completely irrelevant to your content, it will not be of value.

Pitfall #5

Finally, we have backlinks that have anchor texts with no relevant keywords. The text that makes up a back link is hugely important. You don't always have control over it but when you do, make sure to include relevant keyword phrases in the anchor text. This is a very valuable distinction you should focus on when building links.

Black Hat SEO strategies, why to avoid them

Black hat search engine optimization is any technique that marketers use to boost traffic on a website, which the search engines consider unethical. The marketer would either be breaking one or more of the search engine's rules, creating a poor user experience on the website in the attempt to boost traffic, or unethically presenting different content to search engines than to human visitors on their site.

Things to avoid

- **Keyword Stuffing** – long lists of keywords that produce no actual value to the visitors of your site.
- **Invisible Text** – This includes any text that is not immediately visible to an end user but is placed on a page solely for the purpose of the search engine crawler.
- **Doorway Pages** – This is a page that visitors will never see, generally created to get the search engine

spider to index your website a different way in order to boost rankings.

Techniques to building effective links

In order to start building effective back links to your website, you should do your homework. Start by doing some research on your niche.

Build a list of relevant websites in your niche. Find all of your potential competitors even if they don't directly compete with you. For example, as an interior decorator, you can make a list of other interior decorators from cities around where you typically work. You don't directly compete with them, because they work in a different market than you do. Look for forums or blogs talking about the same topics that your website is about. Also look to build a list of directory websites that have other sites from your niche.

Once you have a solid list, find out how well they are all ranking before you work to get your link on a website that might in fact hurt your rankings. To accomplish this, you can find free online Google PageRank checker tools. These sites will typically have one text box where you type the URL of a website and it will return with the Google PageRank score between zero and ten. Typically pages with a PR of zero or one are not worth pursuing. Websites with a PR of two to four are fairly typical and worth investing your time to get your site listed on them. Anything higher than a PR score of four is very valuable and you should work hard to get listed on that site.

Once you know the PR scores, start with the forums and blogs that rank higher. Register to become a member of these websites so that you can start commenting or posting. On a forum type site, read the rules of the forum to see if you are allowed to have a link to your website in your posts. If you don't follow the individual forum's rules they will ban you and delete your posts. Do not focus solely on marketing your website or your services; spend a bit of time contributing to the community, by sharing quality comments or posts about relevant topics to the blog or discussion piece.

After going through the list of forums and blog posts, the next step is to ask your competitors for a link. You can't directly place a link on someone else's website so in this case you will search through their website looking for some sort of contact page. When you find it, you will proceed to send an e-mail or a message to the owner of the website, asking them nicely to consider placing a link somewhere on their website for their visitors. Their answer might be no. However, if you provide valuable content for their visitors, and that is understood by the website owner, more often than not they will create the back link for you on their site.

CHAPTER 11

Press Release Marketing

Press releases are one of the fastest and most effective ways to increase the traffic on your website. They are fairly easy to write. With the help of some of the great syndication services available online, you no longer have to worry about getting them out to news sites on your own.

The content for a press release can be anything that you can write about your business that you believe to be newsworthy. One of the reasons it is more effective than just advertising your product and service, is that most people are addicted to the news. Also, you can generalize that we don't often wilfully like to be advertised to. The basic composition of a press release turns what would have been an advertisement into a piece of news about either your product, service or your business itself.

A properly constructed press release can incorporate a form of sensationalism so as to get the readers excited about what you have to offer.

I am going to share a few amazing resources in this chapter to help you get your press releases out to hundreds if not thousands of news agencies for little or no cost.

One of the great aspects of a press releases is that it can contain links for people reading online to click, which would redirect the readers to any page on your website. If your press release is picked up by one or more news agencies as a worthwhile story, it can both improve your rankings in the search engines for your website and send viral amounts of targeted traffic to your website. It is one of the fastest ways to get a surge of fresh visitors over to your website.

Anatomy of a press release

One of the most important aspects to a good press release is having a compelling and interesting headline. This will catch the attention of both the readers and the news agencies looking to publish new information. If you don't spend significant time to find a compelling headline, you can forget about it bringing any additional visibility to your business.

The next important part to building a great press release is the introduction, or the first three sentences of your text. This is equivalent to meeting someone for the first time and giving them your first impression. You never get a second chance to make a first impression. The same thing applies to writing your introduction for your press release. These three sentences are going to determine if the reader will in fact continue to read the rest of the article or if they are disinterested and will go read something else. You can lose 80% to 90% of your readers if you don't focus on getting their attention in the first few lines.

Finally, you have to write the body of the press release. Always remember that you are not pitching your product or service, instead, you are merely conveying a piece of news. Tell the story about your company's mission or accomplishments. Maybe you can tell them how you have revolutionized your service in your niche. A great strategy is to find other pieces of mainstream news that are current and somehow relate that to your business in your press release. If you can manage to connect your article to current news in any way, you have a much bigger chance of getting picked up by both online and offline news agencies.

It is best to leave the links to your website out of the body of the article. I use the body of the article to primarily focus on creating interesting news and I place the link to my website within the "about" section of the press release. Every press release that you create will have an about section. This is your opportunity to craft an interesting sales pitch about your company. It's where you should share what you do, what you offer, why they should buy from you and what sets you apart from your competitors.

Where do I send my press release

So you've written a killer press release that is sure to get you a spot on CNN or another major news station, but now you need to let them know about it. Not only do you need to get them to know about it but you also need to get them to read it. Hopefully, once they read it, the quality or the article itself will convince them to publish it.

A few years ago, once you had written your press release, you would have to stand in front of your fax machine for hours sending out the same press release to as many different news publications as you could get fax numbers for. The task was daunting and ineffective most of the time. Fortunately, this is no longer the case. With the advancements of technology, coupled with the power of the internet, it can be as simple as just submitting your press release to one of the major news syndication services and voila, your press release is now available to hundreds or even thousands of different news agencies almost immediately. Furthermore, you can schedule the release for a later date if you so choose. That way, if you are leaving on business and you know that something that would be considered newsworthy will happen while you are away, you could easily write the release in advance of your trip and then schedule it to be released while you are away.

Most syndications services also offer extra features, such as advanced analytics, statistics and information about the success of your press release. Some of the syndication websites offer their services for free and others charge you to publish a press release.

There are two major press release syndication services that I will be writing about in this book. In my opinion, they are the only ones you even need to consider: PRLog.org and PRWeb.com.

Both of them are fairly similar in nature, but I will go over the differences in detail, since you might consider using both at different times for your press releases.

PRLog.org is one is one of my favourites and is probably the first one that you will use until you have a bit more experience writing press releases. You should start with them because they offer their services for syndicating your press release completely free of charge. They are relatively easy to get started with. You only need to sign up and fill in your company profile on their site. Once you write your press release, you can send it out with a click of a few buttons on their site. However, they do have certain limitations compared to the paid services that are available. For one thing, they allow you to put a website link in your press release, but they do not allow you to control what the link will be called, which is a tactic for building authority with search engines to get your site ranked higher. Also, their reporting and analytics information is very basic and doesn't do a good job to indicate how effective the article was. However, if you setup the proper tracking services on your website, you will be able to determine if the new traffic that you are receiving came from your press release or not based on how many people clicked one of your links.

PRLog.org does offer a paid option for releasing a press release. Their pricing is not unreasonable at about $50 per release. They offer the ability to include search engine friendly links to your website, as well as a few other features.

The second syndication service is PRWeb.com. This service is quite a bit more impressive when it comes to the list of news agencies subscribed to get their news feeds. They also have a lot more features than PRLog.org. For example, on PRWeb.com (Roggio 2013) you can create press releases in video or audio format. You can also include nice big images and all of the links that you place in your press release are search engine friendly links. For these extra features and services, their base pricing starts at $250 per release and can be as much as $500 for a single release. They do offer bulk pricing if you want to purchase a few at a time.

Ultimately, you will want to use both services at different times. You might consider sending out three free press releases and then one paid one, while tracking the difference in performance between the two.

CHAPTER 12

SMS Marketing

SMS marketing is a rather new and still much underused marketing method, which is exciting for me to share. This concept works really well for brick and mortar businesses, such as stores, shops, or restaurants. It can be used with any other type of business as well.

SMS marketing, sometimes referred to as text message marketing, lies around you building a list of cellular phone numbers of your customers or prospects, by having them opt-in to your list. They are enrolled once they send an SMS message with a specific keyword to a specific number. Once the list is built, you have the opportunity and ability to send a text message in bulk as often as you want.

The real power of SMS marketing is that studies have shown that more than 98% of text messages are opened and read.[7] This provides a huge advantage to small business owners. Another great thing about SMS marketing is that it is really inexpensive to implement. It can cost as little as a few pennies

---

[7] http://www.practicalecommerce.com/articles/4139-Text-Messaging-Effective-for-Retailers-

for each text message sent. Setting up your own campaign is easy, as is building your list. I can't find any downsides to using this form of marketing for your business.

Choosing a service provider

There are lots of different service providers to choose from when it comes to SMS marketing services. The criteria in picking providers are resumed to a few basic things to look for when deciding which company should host your marketing campaign.

The first thing to look for is what is called a vanity number. This is the 5-digit phone number that your subscribers are going to send their initial text message to in order to subscribe to. What would you prefer: asking your customers or prospects to send a text to 74925 or to 88555? Notice how much easier the second number is to remember, to repeat to your prospects and to type into a phone. Having a good vanity number can increase the results of your SMS marketing campaign greatly, but not all service providers have very good numbers to offer.

The second thing to look for is the availability of your preferred enrolment keyword on the vanity number that you chose. The way that the service works is that the phone number that you get is shared with many other companies. What separates your campaign from theirs is your enrolment keyword. An example to this is Dominos Pizza asking their customers to text the word PIZZA to 55566 to sign up for their list. The keyword PIZZA might be available on 74925 but probably won't be available on 55566. Your enrolment keyword should be well thought out in advance of building your campaign and you should find out in advance if it is available on a good vanity number prior to choosing a company to do business with.

Other than those two elements, you should take into consideration the pricing options or plans of the service providers and the cost of running your campaign on their platform. Some companies will charge you a flat monthly fee, plus a charge per text message sent, while others will charge per text message sent. Others, still, will just charge you a certain flat fee for the month and include a set number of available text messages. You need to determine what payment option works best for your marketing campaign.

Let's design your ideal campaign

The great thing about SMS marketing is that it is really easy to build a campaign and doesn't need to take you a lot of time. The few things that you need to determine in building your campaign are:

- **The enrolment keyword** – This is the main keyword that your subscribers will have to send to the 5-digit number in order to subscribe to your list.
- **The purpose of your campaign** – This is where you determine what you are offering to your subscribers and how valuable it will be for them.

- **How often to text** – You need to determine the ideal frequency of marketing messages so as not to upset your subscribers and make them unsubscribe.
- **Your main Offer** – This is where you determine the product or service you are offering to the subscribers of your list.

Your enrolment keyword should be a single word the best describes your business or the campaign that you are running. It should be easy to spell and very easy to remember.

An example of this for a restaurant can be DESERT. The restaurant can ask their patrons to text DESERT to 55566 to get a free piece of pie. In this example, the restaurant is essentially offering a free piece of pie to anyone who leaves their cellular phone number to be marketed to further. Once the restaurant has their phone number, it can send them a weekly message with the specials for that week, for example. If the customer comes back at least one more time to the restaurant and buys any meal, the restaurant will most likely make back all of the missed profit from offering them a free piece of pie. Better yet, that customer will probably tell their friends to come to this restaurant to get a free piece of pie as well. Now the restaurant has their customers doing the advertising for them. Do you see how exciting this method of marketing can be?

When determining the purpose of your campaign, you should always think of how you can provide significant value to your subscribers while asking for nothing in return. You want to entice your subscribers to remain on your list and not to unsubscribe.

Here is an example of a marketing campaign that I can run for my marketing business.

Send a text with the keyword MARKETING to 55566 in order to receive weekly text messages that include incredibly valuable tips, tricks, tactics and techniques to being as effective as you can with marketing your small business.

Notice how I am offering free marketing advice. You have no obligation to remain a subscriber as you can unsubscribe at any point. My intention is to convince you to sign up and read my advice. When you need further help, know that I have services available to help you.

How often you should send a text message will depend on your campaign and your subscribers. If you send messages too often, then you will annoy some of the subscribers and they will take the opportunity to unsubscribe from your list. If you don't send them messages often enough, by the time you finally do send out messages, they won't be effective. If you are providing information or advice in your target area of expertise or your niche, then you should send out text messages more often. I usually like to send text messages to my list once a week. If you are promoting your product or service, then you should probably only send out a message once every two weeks or maybe even once a month. Any campaign that requires you to send out a message at a longer interval than once a month is probably not worth pursuing.

Examples of a campaign: "The top tips to eating healthy delivered to your phone once a week"; "Our company's biggest specials delivered to your phone once a month".

The last part of building your ideal SMS marketing campaign is to determine your main offer. Even if you are offering information or advice and providing a lot of value, you should always send a text message blast every once in a while with a call to action. This is where you will either ask them to come into your storefront, or visit your website. This effort will bring in direct revenue as a result of your SMS marketing efforts.

For example: "Exclusive offer for 50% off my 1-on-1 marketing consultation services if you act today by visiting my website."

How to build your SMS list

There are lots of ways to build your SMS marketing list. Some of them are more effective than others.

I can't write this concept enough throughout this book but if you are offering value, you can always convince people to sign up to your list. Create a compelling campaign where people will naturally be attracted to sign up and receive the text messages.

Offer them an incentive to sign up. The example that I used earlier in the chapter was to offer them a free desert in exchange for them joining your SMS list. You can also offer

10% off the price to one of your services in exchange for them signing up for your SMS list.

If you have a physical location for your business, you should post a sign in a visible location, such as on your front door or possibly right next to the cash register. If you own a restaurant or coffee shop, you can place a sign on tables or on coffee tables if you have a lounge for your customers to wait.

The most effective way to get people to sign up to your list will probably always be to ask each and every one of your customers to sign up verbally. Ask them to do it as a favour. People generally love doing favours, even if they haven't yet built a relationship with you. When you ask them to sign up verbally, your chances of them signing up will significantly increase.

CHAPTER 13

Business card marketing strategies

Yes, you read that correctly. In this chapter I will go over some killer strategies to using business cards effectively.

You would be surprised to know how many business cards are printed in North America each and every year. Unfortunately an incredibly large percentage of them end up in the landfill without being of much use.

Most people who use them don't know how to use them effectively in serving their purpose. I worked long and hard to build a list of creative ways of optimizing this wonderful tool and have it actually work for you.

How to design the best business cards

I probably receive somewhere in the order of hundreds of business cards each and every month. I get them from varied locations. I am very active in the local small business networking scene, in seminars, trade shows, and conferences. If there is one thing I get a lot of, it is business cards.

The point of handing out business cards is getting the other person to offer you their card so that you can follow up with them. However, we all know that most of the time, the majority of cards you receive are not even worth following up with.

Let me share the characteristics that make for a good business card as opposed to one I wouldn't follow up with.

Rules:

- A good card with no call to action is a waste of time. There should be some sort of action to take upon reception of your card. For example, I like to offer a free guide or e-book upon visiting my website.
- Always put links to your social media profiles on your business card. Remember that social media is a way for you to build relationships with your customers and you should take huge advantage of it.
- Never use your Gmail, Yahoo, AOL, Hotmail or any other generic public e-mail service on your business cards. You can purchase a domain name online for less than $10 with yourbusinessname.com. It is so much more professional and it shows that you are serious about being in business.
- Place a QR code on your cards. You can create QR codes with links to your website for free. Just look up QR generator on Google. This will attract more traffic to your website and you will have an opportunity to squeeze their e-mail when they visit your site.
- Have a tagline on your business cards, but try and keep it between 3 to 5 words. Shorter is sweeter and will cause less confusion in conveying your message.

- Always use a good card stock. You don't need to do anything over the top, such as having rounded corners, but don't cheap out on thin card stock. The least you should consider is a 14pt stock. Most printing companies don't even charge more for it.
- Don't use P.O. boxes on your cards. If you want to include a mailing address, then use a real address. If you don't want to put your real address, then you probably shouldn't be placing any address on your cards. If someone needs your address, they will most likely look it up online before trying to find your business card anyway.
- Leave some room on at least one of the sides so that you can write something on your business card. You might either want to include some extra information before handing your card over or the person you give it to might want to write a note about their conversation with you.
- When designing your business card, add value wherever you can. If your card has value, then they won't throw it away. Give some information, include a calendar, and write something by hand on your cards or whatever else you can think of.

If you follow most or all of the rules outlined above, your cards will be more effective when you hand them out to people.

Where to get your business cards printed

There are abundant options when it comes to printing your business cards. You can go to your local Office Depot or Staples center and have them printed. You can get business cards printed at any Kinkos location. You can also purchase business card stock and print them on your home printer.

The problem is that all three of those options are expensive. But wait, how could printing on inexpensive card stock with your own printer be more expensive than having your business cards printed professionally? Well, professional companies offer deals when printing hundreds or thousands of cards. Compared to the amount of ink that you would use for the same result, the cost savings are unbelievable.

Places like Kinkos, Office Depot and Staples charge you way more than you should ever spend for business cards. They will often charge you a lot extra to print in full color; they will charge you to print with bleeds on each side and various other hidden charges and fees.

If you want to start printing in very large quantities, I suggest that you find a printing broker. There are many people whose business is to work for you and bid your printing project against large printing companies to get you the best rate. If you want to print at least 5000 cards this can be a good bet for you.

Ultimately, if you only need somewhere in the range of 500 to 2000 business cards, like most of us, you should use online printing companies.

One of my favourites is called Next Day Flyers. They are currently offering very high quality, inexpensive business card printing solutions and they ship incredibly quickly.

You have the option to design your business card directly on their website using thousands of pictures and templates, or you can upload your own design. They print the cards on high quality 14pt thick card stock and will ship them right to your door within a few days, depending on the shipping option that you choose.

The best part is that you can get about 1000 of these amazing cards printed for under $20. If you'd like to get started with them, use the following link:

http://builditandtheywontcome.com/business-cards

The best strategy for using your business card

This strategy is a real gem. Using this strategy over the last few years has made me so many new customers, that I feel it is something I should share.

Bill Walsh once said, "Always give away your best content for free and people will naturally be attracted to you". Well, this is my best content. I have worked long and hard to develop this technique and I hope you appreciate it.

I was at a chamber of commerce event last week and I engaged in a really great conversation with Julie the accountant. We spoke about various ways to improve her business using many of the marketing strategies outlined in this book. As the conversation was nearing its end I wanted her to have my contact information, so I quickly pulled out my business card, front side up and handed it to her, all the while maintaining eye contact.

She then grabbed the card but I held it as I spoke to her: "Julie, I would like to give you this card but first, I want to do something special for you".

I took it back, hid it from her view and wrote a number on the card, before showing it again.

She reached out once more, but I held on and didn't let go. She smiled at me, confused. "Julie", I said, "what I have just done for you is that I personalized the business card. Nobody else in the world has the same business card as you. I want you to do me a favour and hold onto this card for at least 30 days."

I continued to explain that on the first of every month, I host a contest and that if she visited my website (which is written on both sides of the card), she has a chance to win two movie tickets to see any movie that she wants.

She smiled again, let out a little chuckle and grabbed the card. We then both left our conversation to continue the evening and meet other people.

Now, let's go over what I did in a few steps.

1. I used her name multiple times. To most people, their name is the most sacred word in their vocabulary. It shows that you care about them and not just about the business opportunity.

2. I maintained eye contact throughout the entire process. This helps to build rapport with the potential prospect. Once again, it shows that you care about them.

3. I held onto the card without letting go. This is meant to build a bit of anticipation. Julie was startled that I didn't let go of the card right away.

4. I pulled back the card, explained that I was going to do something special for her, hid the card and wrote a unique number on it. This, once again, is meant to increase the anticipation and create excitement.

5. I then offered the card back, used her name once again, started explaining to her what I had done but then most importantly, I asked her to do me a favour. People love to help others on a subconscious level. Asking them to do you a favour opens them up to listening to you further.

6. I asked her to hold onto my card for at least 30 days. Putting the time constraint is more important than a specific number. She is going to be so much more likely to hold onto my card rather than throwing it out.

7. Then, I then asked her to visit my website and showed her where it is on my card. I took advantage of one more chance to get her to visit my site and to promote to her further or grab her contact details from my website.

8. I mentioned a contest, which adds to the excitement and creates a feeling of competition that people generally tend to like.

9. I offered her something of value in exchange for her contact information. I offered her a chance to win tickets for the movies.

10. The best part of it all is that I created an experience unlike any other while giving a business card. She is likely to remember me for a long while.

If executed properly, this business card exchange should only take about 60 seconds to complete, but will make a world of difference when it comes to your prospects' willingness to do business with you. This phenomenal marketing strategy only costs you approximately twenty dollars per month for the movie tickets, but can make you thousands of dollars of sales in your business.

I have more great strategies for using business cards effectively. In fact, I have so many that I couldn't fit them all in this book and I wanted to make sure to leave room to deliver the rest of the great content I have for you.

To see a video of this business card strategy in action, as well as similar strategies, visit the following website:

http://builditandtheywontcome.com/card-strategy

I want to reward you for reading this book; make sure to enter the following coupon code *biatwc25pct* to save 25% if you choose to purchase my video series on that page.

CHAPTER 14

How to seal the deal, sell to your customers

It basically boils down to two words. I hope you are ready for this.

BE GENUINE

When you aren't being genuine with your customers, they tend to see right through you. They instantly feel that you don't care for them. Your customers need to know, like and trust you before they decide to buy from you. Otherwise, any sales tactic that you use can be considered a form of manipulation.

That's all there is to it. If you show your customer that you are truthful, authentic and in full integrity, they will naturally build a connection with you and will trust that what you are offering is indeed what they need or want. They will trust that you have their best interests at heart and they will trust that you want to help them.

If you follow these guidelines, you can even charge more than your competition and still expect to outsell them by many fold.

The power of influence

Influence is about the art and the complex process of persuasion. When you interact with someone, you are probably doing one of two things. You are either being persuaded to help others or you are persuading others to help you.

Remember, the idea is to remain in full integrity and to be genuine. You should never persuade someone to buy something from you that won't genuinely add value to them.

Now, how do you persuade people to help you reach your goals? Start by setting your goals and making them really clear.

Most salespeople don't even know what they are trying to accomplish when going into a sales opportunity. The easy answer is that they want to sell a product or service in exchange for a profit. If that's your only motivator, it will not be too effective. I'm not saying that you'll never sell anything, but you will probably not be a very good salesperson.

You should figure out a better way to motivate yourself to make the sale. Ultimately, the reason you are selling something is that you are trying to solve a problem for them. Think about your customer and determine in advance how buying what you are selling can help them.

Keeping customer satisfaction in mind, get to know your customers and ask them some questions. Your job is to find out what would motivate them to buy from you and to use that motivation to your benefit.

When you begin to realize that it's about what they want to buy from you and not about what you want to sell to them, you will become a supreme influencer.

The key to persuasion

We can simplify this down to two main customer motivators that all people have. People are either motivated by the desire to gain or they are motivated by the fear of loss.

If you want to be a master persuader, you should master both major motivators.

When entering a sales scenario with your next prospect, figure out what they can gain from your product or service that they are already looking for. I'm not talking about the features of your product; I am referring to the results that you can offer if they purchase from you what they already want to gain.

Determine what your prospects stand to lose if they don't purchase a product or service from you. It's not always black and white. What motivates one customer is not necessarily going to motivate another. You need to look for what that specific customer is afraid to lose by not doing business with you and focus on that. There is no cookie cutter or a one size fits all approach to this.

People are often even more motivated by the fear of loss than they are by the desire to gain. Some of the big fears that you can work with are:

- Fear of loss of anything they've worked hard for
- Fear of disapproval of others
- Fear of financial loss
- Loss of health
- Loss of a loved one
- Loss of the love of someone
- Change / Risk / Uncertainty

Remember never to use their fears in any negative way that may cause them pain. This can be seen as a form of manipulation.

The best way to master the art of persuasion is to show them what they stand to gain, as well as how they can avoid a loss or overcome a fear that they might have. When you can skilfully bring both of these major motivators into one sales scenario, you can be assured of your success.

The Karmic way

Karma can be summed up in one short sentence. What goes around comes around. Whether you believe it or not, this concept can and should also be applied to your business.

Doing business the karmic way involves understanding who you are doing business with. You might be doing business with a partner, coworkers or employees. You might or might not have distributors or suppliers, joint ventures with other companies, people or companies that you outsource work to, and hopefully you do business with customers as well. You should make a list of everyone that you do business with in some way, shape or form.

When you have that list, next to each name, come up with different ways of offering something to them without any expectation of anything in return. If you keep your business relationships happy, they will in turn, according to the rules of Karma, keep you happy.

Some examples of following this would be to:

- Offer your joint venture partners a higher share of the earnings from your partnership than they originally asked.
- Treat your customers with respect and the admiration that they deserve.
- Provide an irresistible offer to your customers that they absolutely wouldn't consider declining.
- Offer your employees your service or product at or under your cost to thank them for their service.
- Empower your partners to make certain key decisions that can ultimately affect the outcome of your business in a big way and trust that they will do it properly.

Obviously, there are more ways of showing people that you do business with your Karmic side. Just keep in mind that if you do good things for others, the universe will pay you back for your efforts. Keep them happy and they will keep you happier. Do for others what you would want them to do for you; treat them exactly as you would like to be treated. You will without a doubt be successful in your efforts.

Selling with Integrity

Finally, in order to really be effective in sealing the deal and selling to your customers, always act in full integrity. If your intention is to swindle them or manipulate them against their will to buy from you, you cannot be successful for very long.

Integrity builds trust and shows honesty. When your customers trust you, they will have no problem buying from you. If they have a reason not to trust you, they typically will take the opposite path and not buy from you.

Many people have a stigma when it comes to the word sales or marketing. They see it as being negative. A limiting belief that most people have is that, since a salesperson has an agenda in mind or stands to gain from selling you something that they can't be objective and sell to you in true honesty.

It is perfectly possible to be incredibly and wildly successful in sales while being honest, sincere, and in full integrity. Wild success in sales will mean big money, getting what you want when you want it all, or at least most, of the time.

However, you have to believe in what you are trying to sell. Your product or service needs to be something that provides significant value to other people. When you are choosing what to sell, make sure that it is something that you honestly believe in. It's even better if it's something that you use yourself! It makes it easier when you can choose to sell something with the "one size fits all" idea. It's not always possible but makes it much easier. Customers relate easily with products if they see others buying the same things. Find something that you are passionate about and get behind that. You should be incredibly enthusiastic and confident when speaking about your product.

Do whatever it takes to learn all the ins and outs of your product or service as best you can. It is so much easier to sell something when you can speak about it freely and answer any questions that might come up. Use the product yourself regularly. This is not always possible but will help make you more successful at marketing it to others if you can honestly say that you use it yourself and have received the value that it has to offer. Find ways to relate the product or service that you are selling to your customer. It is much easier if you can show them that it will interest them or that they can relate to it in some way. Leverage your personal skills when it comes to the product or service that you are selling.

It is important to lay everything on the table when you are trying to sell or market something to someone else. Do not leave anything out when speaking about it. Tell them all the positive facets, but don't leave out the negative aspects or side effects. You need to build a trust relationship or a rapport with your customers, which will prove very beneficial. Do not manipulate your buyer. It's all about building a trusting relationship with the potential customer or prospect. Stay away from the used car sales tactic. Do not keep pushing features or specifications towards your prospect. It just doesn't work.

CHAPTER 15

Bonus: Ways to make money online

Just when I thought I finished this book, I decided to add a bonus chapter. More than 57% of people who start reading a book never actually finish reading it.[8] To thank you for getting this far in my book and to congratulate you, I wrote an extra bonus chapter. It is does not necessarily go in line with the rest of the book, since it's not about marketing your business.

You see, I have used some of these marketing techniques myself for years. I will most likely write a longer, fuller book just on ways to make money online at some point. In the meantime, I want to leave you with a little something to get you started.

Now that you have a strong business with an even stronger marketing plan, you owe it to your business to find and implement new systems for better profit.

Now that you are using the internet to market your business, you can easily implement new strategies and make extra revenue with little effort. Let's get started.

---

[8] http://www.statisticbrain.com/reading-statistics/

How to use Affiliate Marketing

I am excited to share this with you. Once you read about this technique and start implementing it, you won't be able to sleep properly. You will be constantly logging onto your site to see how fast your commissions are coming in.

Affiliate Marketing is the concept of referring customers to someone else's product or service. That company then proceeds to send you a nice commission check for the referral.

One of the reasons that this is so exciting is because you don't have to store products in your garage; you don't need to deliver the service to a customer. You don't need to deal with shipping or fulfillment and best of all; you don't need to worry about angry or screaming customers. The company that you refer the customers to is completely responsible for taking care of all of this on your behalf. It is really easy to setup as well.

Once you sign up to be an affiliate of a site or company, you are provided with a special link that has a unique identifier built into it. When you give out that link to visitors and they click it, it automatically tracks who referred them. For each of their purchases, the affiliate company pays you a referral commission. Sometimes, the company provides you with fancy clickable pictures and banners that you can use on your website.

I like to use this when writing an article in my blog telling my readers how great a product or service is and listing the reasons for using it. Then, I make sure to provide them my affiliate link before they get to the bottom of the page.

Affiliate commission payouts can be either a percentage based on the final sale amount or a fixed dollar amount per order. They vary depending on the company, product or the industry.

It's important that the products or services must be relevant to your site. Find things that complement your business and for which you don't already provide, and sign up as an affiliate to sell their products. You can place pictures or banners around your site. You can write reviews or articles about their product. Videos on YouTube also prove to be effective. Make sure to include the affiliate link in the annotations of the video as well as the description box when uploading your video.

You can also spread your link via properly crafted posts on social media networks. As they often have a tendency of going viral from one moment to the next, they can prove to be very valuable.

Here are two websites for affiliate referral systems that you can sign up with.

- www.commissionjunction.com
- www.clickbank.com

Making money with Pay Per Click

Earlier on in the book, I wrote about pay per click from your businesses perspective and how you can use it to get more traffic to your website. There is also an opposite perspective to this technique. This is the concept of placing other businesses Pay Per Click ads on your website. When your visitors click those ads, you are the one who makes the money.

You don't need to have individual joint ventures with each and every business that advertises on your website, since there are many providers that offer this kind of setup. One of the most well known ones is called Google AdSense. This service takes little more than 10 minutes to sign up for and it can be very lucrative for your business.

The concept involves you signing up on the Google AdSense page and then creating your ad unit. All you need to do is provide details about the amount of space you have available to display ads on your website. Once you choose a size, Google will provide you with a source code to copy and paste into your website. If you are having trouble to set that up, please don't hesitate to contact any web development company and they should be able to help you set that up for very little cost.

Once the code has been installed, Google analyses the pages on which you placed the code and tries it's best to provide advertisements that are relevant to the content within. For example, if you were writing about nutrition on your website, you might see an advertisement about vitamins.

When visitors come to your website and see your content, should they choose to click on the advertisements that Google placed on your page, you will earn money. Google has an algorithm to determine the value of the content provided on your page. If you add more value, you will earn more money per click; the visitors of your website will not even need to buy anything on the re-directed website.

To see this in action, please feel free to visit my website at http://www.kwik-web.com and browse around through different web pages. The advertisement is on the right hand side in the sidebar. Notice how on different pages the advertisement changes automatically to match the contents of that page.

Create more Products, Make more Money

If you create more products, you have the opportunity to sell more products and when you sell more products, you make more money. The trick is that you should create products that don't require your time or effort to fulfil.

These types of products are usually referred to as information products. What better type of product could you provide in an era known as the information age?

Information products are typically delivered in digital format and can include many of the following:

- E-Books
- Whitepapers
- Video Tutorials
- Written Books
- Access to an E-Course
- Live or Recorded Webinars

- Teleseminars
- Membership Sites

You can create an information product by putting together knowledge that you hold into one or more of the formats from the list above. Then package it to be delivered to the client.

Once the product has been created, you don't have to do anything else except market it. There are no costs to produce more copies of it. There is no packaging and shipping necessary since it's delivered online. Also, the whole thing can be automated really easily from your website. Your customers can go to your site, add the product to their shopping cart, checkout and have the links to download the product instantly without your involvement.

Sometimes, all it takes to create a product is to host one webinar and record its contents. Then with a bit of editing and polishing, you could package it with a copy of your slides. You can have it transcribed by a professional transcription service fairly inexpensively and add that to the package as well. You can add some fill-in-the-blank worksheets to go along with the video as well. Now you have an effective information product ready to market and sell.

Information products can vary in price range; however the majority of them are valued between $200 and $3000 per customer download. Once it's created and the platform to sell it has been set up, it becomes passive income every time you make a sale.

How to monetize your lists

Throughout this book, I mention that you need to create value for potential customers in order to build your list, which you can essentially build through social media marketing platforms, either with followers or with people who join your e-mail marketing list.

When your list grows to an interesting amount of individuals, it becomes valuable to other people.

Here are some things that you can do with your list to monetize it. First off, you can just outright sell your list to another company. There is no real science to figure out its value. Look at the quality of the members on your list and estimate its value compared to what the purchaser is willing to pay for those leads.

I generally don't like selling lists outright, because when I sign up to an e-mail newsletter, I don't want my information passed around to another party.

Instead of selling the list outright, you can sell access to the list. This is my preferred method of monetizing my list, because I have more control over what goes on with the list and I can decide if I agree with the text before it's sent out. I can assure that the e-mail passes a certain level of quality control before sending it out to my subscribers.

Selling access to the list involves finding a person or another company that has an interest in the members of your marketing list and wants to get access to it. Once you have found them, you form a mini joint venture and you offer them access to send e-mail on their behalf to your list. You can charge either a one-off price for sending out that e-mail, or you can charge a commission based on whatever is sold to your audience, through a properly tracked link in that e-mail.

Once again, this might sound complicated. I can assure you that it is easy to implement. If you don't want to do any of these things or just don't know where to start, feel free to contact me and I will be glad to show you how to make it happen.

WORKS CITED

Internet World Stats. *World Internet Usage And Population Statistics.* June 30, 2012. http://www.internetworldstats.com/stats.htm (accessed 01 30, 2013).

Roggio, Armando. *Text Messaging Effective for Retailers.* 08 09, 2013. http://www.practicalecommerce.com/articles/4139-Text-Messaging-Effective-for-Retailers- (accessed 09 14, 2013).

Smith, Craig. *By the Numbers: 64 Amazing Facebook Stats.* 12 28, 2013. http://expandedramblings.com/index.php/by-the-numbers-17-amazing-facebook-stats/ (accessed 01 16, 2014).

Statistics Brain. *Reading Statistics.* 04 28, 2013. http://www.statisticbrain.com/reading-statistics/ (accessed 05 13, 2013).

Vellante, David. *Revisited: The Rapid Growth in Unstructured Data.* 08 17, 2010. http://wikibon.org/blog/unstructured-data/ (accessed 02 12, 2013).

Whois Source. *Internet Statistics.* 01 12, 2013. http://www.whois.sc/internet-statistics/ (accessed 01 12, 2013).

Wikipedia. *CAN-SPAM Act of 2003.* 01 03, 2014. http://en.wikipedia.org/wiki/CAN-SPAM_Act_of_2003 (accessed 01 04, 2014).

STAY IN TOUCH

Visit our website at:
www.BuildItAndTheyWontCome.com

To get a list and links to all resources found in this book.

For more information about Jason, to follow his writing and for links to various programs that he recommends,

stay connected via Jason's social media pages:

 facebook.com/jchechik

 twitter.com/jasonchechik

 linkedin.com/in/jasonchechik

27124536R00083

Made in the USA
Charleston, SC
27 February 2014